PRAISE FOR

Praying Naked
The Spirituality of Anthony de Mello, S.J.

"*Praying Naked* is about awakening. Awakening to the treasures within you. Father Stroud says he's not trying to change your life, simply pointing to the treasures inside you. But, of course, if you constantly realize how rich you are within, your life will change of itself. This book should carry a health warning: it could change your life—for the better."
—Peter de Rosa, author of *Rebels: The Irish Rising of 1916*

"Vast numbers of people have already benefited from Father Stroud's teaching of the spirituality developed by Reverend Tony de Mello; and vastly more can benefit from reading Father Stroud's new book."
—Sir John M. Templeton, spiritual philanthropist
and founder of the Templeton Fund

"This fascinating book is an excellent choice for those who yearn for spiritual happiness, self-discovery, and self-awareness."
—Thomas Murphy, former president of Capital Cities ABC, Inc.

"This enlightening book captures Tony de Mello's wit together with his spiritual insights. Reading it will enhance your life. It is an owner's manual for the spiritual human being."
—Peter O'Malley, former owner of the Los Angeles Dodgers

"I loved *Praying Naked*. Father Stroud's reflections on the spirituality of Anthony de Mello are filled with humor and wisdom. He shows us how to be calm, to be accepting, and to be loving, but more important, he just shows us how 'to be.' Father Stroud enhances his insights with excellent anecdotes, quotations, and exercises. If you enjoy this book as much as I do, you'll be quoting from it often."
—Carmen Finestra, producer of ABC's *Home Improvement* and
president of Wind Dancer Production Group

"At some point in every life it's only the inner path to growth that matters. Father Francis Stroud's *Praying Naked* provides all the mapping you will need along that path."
—Norman Lear, executive producer of *All in the Family*
and seventeen other major TV productions

The Spirituality of
Anthony de Mello, S.J.

IMAGE BOOKS

DOUBLEDAY

New York   London   Toronto   Sydney   Auckland

praying
naked

J. Francis Stroud, S.J.

AN IMAGE BOOK
PUBLISHED BY DOUBLEDAY
a division of Random House, Inc.

IMAGE, DOUBLEDAY, and the portrayal of a deer drinking from a stream
are registered trademarks of Random House, Inc.

Book design by Caroline Cunningham

Library of Congress Cataloging-in-Publication Data
Stroud, J. Francis.
Praying naked : the spirituality of Anthony de Mello, S.J. / J. Francis Stroud.
p.   cm.
Includes bibliographical references.
1. Spiritual life—Catholic Church. 2. De Mello, Anthony, 1931– I. Title.
BX 2350.3.S77 2005
248.4'82—dc22
2004064940

ISBN 0-385-51314-3
PRINTED IN THE UNITED STATES OF AMERICA

October 2005
First Image Books Edition
1 3 5 7 9 10 8 6 4 2

This book is the result of years of study of the work of Anthony de Mello, S.J. My own association with him, my reading of his books, listening to his presentations, producing television programs and tape recordings with him have all contributed to what is contained herein.

However, if there is one person who has made Tony's approach to spirituality come alive in my own life, I would have to say that I am indebted to—more than anyone else—Tony's dearest and closest friend, Dick McHugh, S.J. Dick confronted Tony with his own clay feet and probably more than anyone else made him the fine spiritual teacher he was. Dick has relentlessly done the same for me. As much as I resented this at the time of its happening, I stand today ever grateful to him for his honesty and abiding friendship. It is hard for me to distinguish between the values imparted to me by Tony de Mello and the painful growth afforded me over the years by Dick McHugh.

For this reason, with heartfelt gratitude, I dedicate this book to Dick McHugh, S.J.

Of course, there are others who have made this work possible. I couldn't write this dedication without mentioning Jonathan Galente. No one has made my life and work easier, more enjoyable, and more productive than Jonathan. Only he and God know the depth of my gratitude. I also thank my helpers in locations around the world, who assist in organizing and presenting de Mello conferences. And I thank all who helped prepare the physical manuscript of this book, including writer-editor Carole Spearin McCauley for her capable services.

—J. Francis Stroud, S.J.
Fordham University, New York

Contents

Foreword

This book has been written in response to the many requests for an organized approach to a spirituality that has helped numerous people, including myself, in a day and age when we are bombarded with the distractions of a frenetic culture. This is a book for those of us who would like to get ourselves on track toward a path that leads us serenely to our Maker.

When the man about whose spiritual approach this book is mainly concerned was asked by a television interviewer, "Why do so many people want to hear what you have to say?," his answer was right to the point. "I think," Tony de Mello said, "what people want is an experience of God."

So many of us want to discover answers to the important spiritual questions, such as "Who am I?" "How do I find true happiness in my life now?" "What is the best way to understand suffering and deal with it?" These are very practical questions, and that is what genuine spirituality deals with. Practicality.

The approach to spirituality found in this book has transformed my own life and, from what I am told, has done the same for countless others. In the numerous conferences that Dick McHugh, S.J., and I have offered in so many countries throughout the world, the response has been so gratifying. It is a pleasure to make this material available to you in a book.

To reap the enormous benefits, to enjoy the spiritual rewards, you needn't give up your business, your home, or your friends. You don't have to ascend a mountaintop and spend hours in contemplation. The emphasis here will be on the gifts and treasures already at work in you by God's grace. If you become *aware* of these, then this book will have fulfilled its purpose.

The journey you start with this book is pleasant, beautiful, and in some ways challenging. I wish you success on it, and Godspeed.

Introduction

The title of this book, *Praying Naked,* is intended to be eye-catching, even humorous. It is certainly not meant to be disrespectful, especially since the book deals with so beautiful a topic as spirituality. The title derives from a real-life situation, as you will soon see. My original plan was to give what is now the subtitle, *The Spirituality of Anthony de Mello, S.J.,* top billing. *Praying Naked,* with its inviting nuance, still stands. Yet the thrust of the book remains Tony de Mello's provocative approach to spirituality.

When dealing with meditation, this book will help you:

- Resolve all the problems presented by our programming and conditioning

- Learn this art of meditation quickly, easily, even in so short a time as three minutes

After I offered this method in a spirituality conference, I was approached by a young woman (easily six months' pregnant) who told me that she practiced this form of meditation frequently. She told me of a very religious aunt who lived with her, who would sit with a very large prayer book on her lap. The aunt would complain, "With all the running around you do, cleaning the house, caring for the children, preparing meals, when do you ever get time to pray?"

So she told this very religious aunt of hers, "I pray when I go into the shower and I focus my attention on my breath, the sounds of the water cascading from the spigot hitting the floor, the sensations I feel as the water runs down my back, and so forth. When I finished, my very religious aunt with the large prayer book on her lap said to me, 'You mean you pray naked!' "

"Thank you, my dear," I replied, "you have just given me the title for my book." I couldn't think of a better de Mello–flavored title to introduce his ideas on spirituality. In actual fact, Tony would have been more conservative in his title selection. He would have loved telling that story publicly, but when it came to print, he was more often than not quite discreet. Ideally, I don't have to be that proper. My reputation is not at stake!

Another reason for the appropriateness of the title: Pope John Paul II wrote, "During the conclave [in which a new Pope is elected] Michelangelo must teach them [the Cardinals]—do not forget: all things are naked and open be-

When I pray for something, I do not pray.
When I pray for nothing, I really pray.

—TONY DE MELLO

———————

The greatest revolution of our generation is
the discovery that human beings, by changing
the inner attitudes of their minds, can change the
outer aspects of their lives.

—WILLIAM JAMES

fore His [God's] eyes." When Michelangelo painted *The Last Judgment* for the Sistine Chapel, all the figures were nude. The fresco was controversial from the moment it was completed, in 1541. He was ordered to cover up the nude figures, but he refused. The Church council had da Voltera, one of Michelangelo's disciples, put *bragh* (underpants) on them. During restoration work in the 1990s, the *bragh* were removed. "Michelangelo was right," says the art history professor Paolo Coloni. "Nakedness is a symbol of *purity* [italics mine]. But what the Pope [John Paul II] said is a contradiction with what the Church had done to the picture through the centuries."

Isn't that interesting? Could it be that the current preoccupation with sex clouds the "purity" of nakedness and sees evil where there is only good?

Another confirmation of my choice of a title occurred when I engaged in conversation with a porter while waiting for transportation from an airport in the South. This man, a very intelligent and deeply spiritual black man, a southern Baptist by religious affiliation, replied to my concern regarding the appropriateness of the title *Praying Naked* for a book on spirituality, saying, "It is a beautiful title. Whenever you stand before God in prayer, you must stand stripped of everything— your possessions, your ego, your clothes. It is a very beautiful title."

I left him with my conviction intact. It is the right title. And I make bold to say Tony de Mello would like it as applied to his thrust of spirituality.

The book presents Anthony de Mello's approach to spirituality that has touched the lives of so many people, bringing those who were disenchanted with their original faith back to their Church with renewed vitality and those who are Christian and non-Christian a view of spirituality that has been extraordinarily enriching in their lives. Over the years, when Tony was alive, I not only arranged his conference schedule in the United States, but I attended most of them and have tried to relay faithfully the themes he so often proposed in those conferences.

Nowadays, when Jonathan Galente and I present these spirituality conferences, the events are enriched by Jonathan's contribution. My part is to present the themes that were offered so marvelously by Tony with his deep insight, his wonderful sense of humor, and his exquisite storytelling. Jonathan integrates these themes into the lives of the conference participants with his exercises.

Our experience of giving these conferences over the past ten years has been very gratifying. I felt it imperative to put into print most of what we do. My own life has been blessed and expanded simply by communicating what Tony gave, as have the lives of the hundreds if not thousands of people who have experienced his approach. I know that you will enjoy reading and thinking about what he offered.

I have added a few personal embellishments to Tony's spiritual principles that I have received from gifted and scholarly people, such as Dr. Deepak Chopra, a well-known medical doctor and lecturer with whom Father Dick McHugh, S.J., and I did a de Mello conference in New York in 1994; Tony Robbins, an extraordinary motivator; Joan Borysenko (whom you cannot help but admire as you listen to her insightful taped presentations or read her books); John Bradshaw, a gifted lecturer; and many others. Assembling the materials has been a joy.

I hope you enjoy reading this book as much as I have loved and been honored to write it.

A neurotic is someone who worries about things in the past that never happened. Not like us normal people who only worry about things in the future that won't happen.

—TONY DE MELLO

one

The de Mello
Three-Minute Meditator

Meditation offers five advantages or rewards:

1. Meditation helps you to live in the present. It eliminates the tendency to relive now not only all the ills of the past, such as resentments, guilt, fears, but even the good experiences of the past. Tony de Mello described it graphically by saying that when something good happens to you, you tuck it away in your little silver box and then, instead of enjoying the present moment (which is new, energizing, and exciting), you stop and look into your little silver box and contemplate nostalgically those past happy times. God forbid you should ever lose your silver box that you carry around with you all the time: an unnecessary piece of baggage.

2. Meditation gives you a direct experience of your self. We create so many false selves, which later we will call primary ego defenses. Then we identify with these false selves. For example, when as a little boy you are pushed around, you find that by pushing back, you are given a little respect, so you do it more often. Finally you get the reputation of being a bully, so you think of yourself as such. Another example: You find that as a little girl, if you snuggle up to your father or grandmother, you get the candy or whatever else you wanted. Soon you think being a coquette is not so bad. As you grow older, the same process takes place when you become a doctor or a bishop or the CEO of your company. It is almost impossible to know who the true "you" really is. Meditation helps by giving you a direct experience of your self. The happy result of this experience is that you eliminate the two major causes of suffering in life: isolation and loneliness. No longer do you feel separate and alone, but united and connected, which, of course, is the basis of love.

3. Meditation quiets down the interior dialog, the inner chatter that goes on in the brain all the time. This quieting down enables you to get in touch with your emotions, with anger, grief, and love. And it is crucial, because if you don't have the ability to feel your emotions genuinely or if you deny these feelings when you have them, they will show up somewhere else through alcoholism, obesity, sexual dysfunction, and sometimes even worse.

4. Meditation alleviates all addictions, such as alcoholism, drug use, and overeating, because it helps you achieve what you are seeking through these addictions. We don't overeat because we need this food. There is something missing in our lives and we try

to fill up that missing part by eating. <u>Meditation helps you to love yourself</u>. This is best illustrated by a story, entitled "Don't Change," found in de Mello's book *Song of the Bird*. It is worth quoting here since it will be referred to several times in the book.

> I was a neurotic for years. I was anxious, depressed, and selfish. Everyone kept telling me to change. I resented them and agreed with them, and I wanted to change, but simply couldn't, no matter how hard I tried. What hurt the most was that, like the others, my best friend kept insisting that I change. So I felt powerless and trapped. Then, one day, he said to me, "Don't change. I love you just as you are." Those words were music to my ears: "Don't change. Don't change. Don't change. . . . I love you as you are." I relaxed. I came alive. And suddenly I changed! Now I know that I could never change till I found some one who would love me whether I change or not!

5. Even well-known doctors like Deepak Chopra from La Jolla, California, and Herbert Benson from Harvard University attest to the benefits of meditation for health. Chopra says in his conference, "Journey to the Boundless," that it is the most valuable thing you can do in your life.

THE MEDITATION METHOD

This exercise, though short, will illustrate the Three-Minute Meditation Method. In the shower (after you have finished

Take a lesson in calmness from children: Watch how they live every moment for the pleasure of the moment.

—PAUL WILSON, *THE LITTLE BOOK OF CALM*

Stress—the worst enemy of health. The number-two emotional response to stress is laughing. The number-one response to stress is . . . crying.

washing), be aware, first of all, of your breathing. Is it shallow, medium, or deep? Breathe only through your nose. Don't try to control it, just be aware of its quality. This is a brief exercise, but if you do it consistently, you will feel its benefits almost immediately. Later, in a sitting or squatting position, you will want to extend the meditation to five or ten minutes more. This will be the beginning of a practice of meditation that will last you a lifetime and provide you with enormous benefits.

Then gently shift your attention to the sounds you hear: the water coming from the spigot, the gurgling of the water going down the drain. You will notice a number of different sounds, sounds you paid scant attention to before, such as the sound of water splashing on the floor. Simply be aware of them all.

How long should you do this? Don't worry about it. Just do it briefly. It probably will take no more than a minute. Next shift your focus to the sensations of the water hitting your head and neck, then your back. Feel it running down your legs, onto your feet. Be aware of your feet touching the floor.

If you have put your hands on the wall, notice each finger touching the marble or tile.

Finally, return to the awareness of your breathing. Be aware of only three breaths. That will end the exercise.

Here are some sincere words of encouragement, as you begin reading this book. So often we do so much for others, our whole lives are spent taking care of others. That is why congratulations are in order. For once you are doing something for *yourself*. And the reason this matters is that, of all creation, *you* have an extraordinary power.

Life is 10 percent things that happen to you and 90 percent how you react to the 10 percent.

Plants have laws that govern their existence. Animals' lives are directed by instinct. No one draws a map for the birds to go south. A squirrel has never experienced the winter yet knows how to hide chestnuts for the cold months ahead.

Yet even animals do not have what you have: the power to create your own world. You do this by adopting an attitude. When you wake up in the morning, you are able to create your day by adopting an attitude of cheerfulness. You can say, "This is going to be a wonderful day." And you know what? It will be. No matter what happens, it *will* be a wonderful day. Try it now. See if it isn't true.

IMPROVING YOUR SELF-IMAGE: FOUR STEPS

Earl Nightingale, a famous radio motivator, once had lunch with Maxwell Moltz, the author of *Psychocybernetics,* and said to him, "Max, I know that we are bounded, even limited in our accomplishments by our own self-image. But is there any way to improve or expand our self-image, our self-concept?"

Maxwell Moltz replied, "Of course." And he outlined a four-point plan that he used to improve self-image. I was amazed that this plan came from a scientist and not from a clergyman. Listen to these steps.

Step 1. Forgive everyone.

Get rid of all those resentments that you have carried around all these years. Just forgive everyone, and watch all that weight fall from your psychological shoulders. You not only feel

Just remember, yesterday is history, tomorrow is mystery, and today is a present, a gift from God.

lighter, you actually feel happy with yourself. You feel you are much bigger than these little hurts. Hence, your image of yourself goes up, increases.

Tony de Mello tells the story of two monks, an older and a younger one, going on a journey. When they came to a small river they saw a beautiful woman sitting on the bank of the river. When the older monk asked the lady what her problem was, she replied, "I want to get to the other side of the river but I cannot swim." The older monk said, "I'll solve that." He put the woman on his shoulders and carried her across the river.

When the monks continued their journey, the younger one complained bitterly. "Do you realize the occasion of sin that you have placed yourself in by carrying that woman across the river?" And later he continued, "Can you imagine the scandal this will create in the monastery, when they hear?" After about an hour of this diatribe the older monk paused in his journey, looked directly at the younger monk, and said, "Son, I left that woman at the bank of the river an hour ago. You are still carrying her with you." •

Step 2. Forgive yourself. (And this is even harder than Step 1.)

Learn to look into a mirror and say, "Don't change, I love you just as you are."

This is the basis of Step 2. You can do it for yourself. Look into a mirror and imagine a dark cloud around your heart. (This cloud is the painful part of your life.) When you breathe in, breathe that dark cloud into yourself, and breathe out in its place your joy, your peace, your serenity, your happiness.

If I were to search for the central core of difficulty in people as I have come to know them, it is that in the great majority of cases they despise themselves, regarding themselves as worthless and unlovable.

—Dr. Carl Rogers

Tong Lang.

Continue breathing in and out. Do it not only for yourself, but for others as well, and see what a difference it will make in your life.

Here's an example. There's a magnificent meditational practice from Tibet called Kundalin. Joan Borysenko once suggested it at a conference in Boston. She described how the Dalai Lama responded when asked how he felt about the Chinese (who murdered the priests, raped the nuns, practically destroyed Tibetan civilization in order to break the will of the people). His response was <u>"I try to take in their pain and give</u> <u>back my joy and peace."</u>

Step 3. *Always see yourself at your best. Expect the best in yourself.*

This step I want to emphasize. When you read this book, sim-ply <u>expect that you will be the best when you have finished.</u> One of the golden keys to success is to act as if failure were impossible. This way you override all the negativity that has been drummed into your subconscious. You were inundated with it from your culture, your parents and teachers, your neighbors, and your education (not to mention your religion, which is one of the greatest programmers and conditioners we have, despite its enormous benefits).

How often did you come home from school with an A on your report card to be greeted with "Why not an A+?" We are simply not good enough! Always expect the best of your-self. This posture of expectancy will actually move you in the direction of what's best in you. And it will start happening to you the day you try it.

There was a story in the news about a little girl who was

There is a need of staggering magnitude for doing something in our educational program to help children and youth acquire realistic attitudes of self-acceptance.

—Dr. Arthur Jersild

unable to smile because the muscles in her face wouldn't respond. The doctors operated, and happily she is able to smile today. It is a known medical fact that exercising the muscles of the face employed in smiling can have a salutary effect on the rest of your well-being. Your life really is directed by your subconscious mind most of the time. What you are doing is planting the seed of cheerfulness in your subconscious mind, where it will have its effect during the day.

Step 4. Stop comparing yourself with others. Go at your own pace.

Some will be ahead, some behind. Just go at your own speed.

A further way to program anything you desire into your subconscious is simply to breathe in deeply and then relax your entire being and say, *Relax now.* Do it a second time, and then a third time. Then breathe three times and say, *Wide awake now.* Then do the breathing and relaxing, and when you are completely relaxed, suggest to yourself that today you remain cheerful no matter what happens. Watch how your subconscious mind will operate even when difficult things occur during the day.

An interesting footnote to this point was made by Norman Cousins (author of *Anatomy of an Illness*) in an interview he had with Tony Robbins in Tony's "Power Talk" series. Cousins described students who took blue and red pills, one a super calmer, one a super exciter, but the contents were reversed. The students were told that the blue pills had the chemicals that produced calm. (Really the red pills had the calming chemicals.) Fifty percent of the students experienced what their expectations led them to believe, proving that mind was more powerful in these instances than was the drug. Of course, this is the principle underlying the use of placebos in medical practice.

Another variation on this idea is Tony's story of the teachers who were told by professional examiners that the students they would teach were "spurters," children who would advance very quickly in their lessons. The professionals had determined this by the tests they had given. At the end of the term, when the professionals returned to check the results, sure enough, those students designated as spurters had advanced rapidly. But the professionals admitted that the results of the tests were doctored. There were no spurters. The children advanced because their teachers "expected" them to advance. And of course this expectation was transmitted to the students continually throughout the term.

TAPPING INTO YOUR OWN TREASURES

Everything you read in this book has been written to emphasize your strengths. I am reminded of the great story of Russell Herman Conwell. He was born in 1843, became an editor, a teacher, a clergyman. One day some young people asked him to offer them some college-level classes, because they couldn't afford to go to college. He envisioned that it would be wonderful to start a college for capable, willing, yet financially indigent youngsters. So he went around the country giving talks in order to raise the money, which eventually was used to build Temple University, in Philadelphia.

One of his stories on his lecture tour was this:

A farmer in Australia heard that other farmers had sold their little farms, gone off prospecting for diamonds, and had become very wealthy. He couldn't wait to do the same. Finally he found a buyer, took the money, and started prospecting for diamonds. At the end of one month, nothing happened, then three months, fruitless, then six months, no success. Finally after a year of fruitless effort, he became so despondent that he jumped off a bridge and committed suicide.

Meanwhile, back on the farm, the man who bought the acreage from the farmer invited a friend over for dinner one night. His friend was admiring a rock that was on the mantelpiece. He was astounded. It was the largest diamond he had ever seen. The farmer said, "I just found that in the stream on our property. We have acres of them all over the place!" The diamonds were unrecognizable because they were in rough, uncut form.

The moral of the story is simple. The first farmer went in search of diamonds everywhere, whereas he was sitting on them at home all the time. Also, even if he saw them, he wouldn't recognize them because they were in a form he wasn't familiar with. They were uncut.

The thrust of this book is not about changing your life but about pointing out the treasures you already possess but don't recognize.

When Michelangelo or Rodin first looked at a piece of marble, they saw not plain stone but a perfect image of the

Each human life has the potentiality of becoming a work of art.

—IRA PROGOFF

Pietà or *The Kiss*. Then their hands went to work to bring out of that marble the beautiful sculpture that already existed there, the one that was simply imprisoned, waiting to be released.

There is a superb creation existing within you. Like an artist, you too are able to release that extraordinary person imprisoned within you.

The first question is: How do we do this? How do we get out of this insane existence in which we now live to enjoy a life of serenity, peace, joy, and happiness?

There will be no attempt here to change your life. The truly effective spiritual masters simply point out all those beautiful treasures that already exist within you. The theme you hear from all of them is: "If any good comes from what I say, *you* did it; if there is any damage, *you* did it." As they say in the East, "The nature of the rain is the same. It grows roses in the garden and thorns in the marshes." A true guru *(gu* = darkness, *ru* = light, hence one who leads you from the ignorance of darkness into the light of understanding) dances his own dance, sings his own song. You do the rest.

The first step to tapping into your own treasures and resources is to understand that the world we have been taught to take for granted—in which we think it perfectly natural to feel elated when someone compliments us or depressed when someone criticizes us, to be worried about our children, to experience tension and stress in our business or work—is wrong. We have to understand that these reactions are "insane," despite the fact that we are told to accept them as "perfectly normal."

In this crazy world, our lives resemble a bus tour. We have all these beautiful sights outside—mountains, sky, clouds,

Seek not abroad. Turn back into thyself, for in the inner man [person] dwells the truth.

—St. Augustine, *City of God*

streams, lakes, and oceans—but we have pulled down all the shutters on the windows. Throughout the journey we spend our time arguing who is going to sit in the front seat. Our lives and energies are spent, exhausted over trivialities: "Will we have enough money to buy a house, a car? How will we educate our children? Where will we live? Should I take this job or that?"

Not that these concerns are unimportant. Sometimes as we sit in that front seat, concerns over business, family, and home are important. But not at the expense of life itself! These concerns fade into insignificance when compared to what you are missing. As Thomas Carlyle once said, "The tragedy of life is not how much we suffer. But how much we miss!"

Even John Lennon, one of the Beatles, echoed this thought when he said, "Life is what happens to us while we are busy making other plans."

So the question persists, "How do we escape this insane world we have been taught to live in and enjoy the real world that is rich in happiness and peace?"

That is what spirituality is all about. It is about "waking up."

Waking up from a trance that has been socially induced. A life hypnosis. It's like being drugged, shot up with heroin from your infancy, and then told that there is a much better life than the one you are experiencing. But now all you want is your drug!

One of the drugs we have all been injected with from our earliest days is the drug of "approval." We constantly seek it. When it doesn't come, especially from our "significant others," we crawl on our knees in order to get it.

It is not easy to wake up, to access this reality. It's like the man who goes into his son's bedroom and says, "Jaime, you must get up. It is time for you to go to school." His son complains, "I don't want to go to school. I hate school. It's dull and boring. And besides, all the kids pick on me." Then the father says, "All right. You have given me three reasons why you don't want to go to school. I will give you three reasons why you ought to go.

"One, it's your duty. Two, you are forty-eight years old. And, three, you are the headmaster!"

No one likes to wake up, to move from that comfortable bed.

WAKING UP: GETTING INTO
THE PRESENT

Are the means of waking up esoteric, mysterious, difficult to discover? Do you have to travel far? Spend your days on a mountaintop, gazing at your belly button?

I remember once walking in a little town called Lonavla in India. My watch had stopped, so I went into a barn and asked the man who was milking a cow what the time was. He lifted the udder of the cow and replied, "It's four o'clock." I was amazed. I told my companion that I was going to test him again. Fifteen minutes later I went in and asked him the time. Again he lifted the udder of the cow and said, "It is four-fifteen." I couldn't get over it. I said, "How can you tell time by simply lifting the udder of a cow?" He said, "I have to lift it if I want to see the clock on the wall in the back!"

Silly little story, isn't it? But it makes a good point. There is nothing mysterious about waking up. It is plain common sense.

◦ Once the Buddha was asked, "Could you sum up your teaching on enlightenment [waking up] in one sentence?" He is said to have replied, "I can sum it up in one word!" "And what is that word?" "<u>Awareness</u>," replied the Buddha. "Could you elaborate on that?" he was asked.

"Of course," replied the Buddha. "<u>Awareness is awareness is awareness</u>."

The spiritual quest, Tony de Mello loved to say, is a journey without distance. "You travel from where you are right now to where you have always been. From ignorance to recognition, for all you do is see for the first time what you have always been looking at.

"Whoever heard of a path that brings you to yourself, or a method that makes you what you have always been? And yet, spirituality, after all, is only a matter of becoming what you really are."

This section on meditation could well begin with the story of Helen Keller. Before the illness that left her blind, deaf, and unable to speak, she was adorable. But when she got older she lived an isolated life, surviving on her instincts very much as an animal would. In fact, she acted so much like a little animal, stuffing food into her mouth, running anywhere she pleased, bumping into walls, furniture, and people, that her parents were about to institutionalize her.

As a final resort, they brought in Annie Sullivan to see what she could do. Annie tried to communicate by teaching her sign language, but as hard as she tried, it just didn't penetrate. Helen thought it was just a game, a silly one at that, and

What lies beyond us and what lies before us are
tiny matters when compared to what lies within us.

—RALPH WALDO EMERSON

seemed to hate it. Finally that extraordinary moment happened, celebrated on stage and screen in *The Miracle Worker,* when at the water pump Helen finally had the breakthrough and realized that what was being signed "w-a-t-e-r" was actually this cool liquid flowing over her hand. With that realization, her life was transformed. She became one of the outstanding women of the twentieth century. In her autobiography, years later, Helen described this moment of "enlightenment" of waking up to the meaning of Annie's signing as the most exhilarating experience of her life. It began the incredible transformation of the wild and undisciplined child into the extraordinary woman she became.

Major points of the story:

1. We all need an Annie Sullivan in our life—someone who will patiently endure our resistance to living in the real world.
2. The breakthrough comes unannounced.
3. It is totally transforming.

During a television interview, Tony was asked about praying. Because he was asked this frequently, in his book *Sadhana* he said he was surprised so many people found prayer difficult when really it was so easy. On television he offered some examples. If you examine these exercises, you notice that they all try to get the "pray-er" or the meditator into the present. For example, he would say, "Feel your back on the chair, your thighs on the edge of your seat, your feet in your shoes." In a sense that is what all teachers of prayer try to do, to get you to live in the present where God is. He is not in the past or in

Muddy waters let stand become clear.

—TONY DE MELLO

the future, which don't exist, but in the present. So if you can get into the present, you can easily get in touch with God, your higher power, or whatever you want to call "God."

Even if you feel you are distracted, you can use these distractions (which are not that bad, as I will show) to get you into the present. For example, this morning while I was meditating, I considered putting this idea of getting into the present down on paper—an act which at that time was in the future, not real; but then I noticed the fact that I was thinking this thought. Becoming aware of thinking is very much an act of the present, so I used a distraction to get myself into the present, simply by becoming aware of it.

Another story that illustrates the effect that meditation has on a person tells of the ascetic who would not eat or drink before sundown every day. In what seemed a sign of heavenly approval for his austerities, a bright star shone on top of a nearby mountain, visible to everyone in broad daylight, though no one knew what brought the star there.

One day the man decided to climb the mountain. A little village girl insisted on going with him. He urged the child to drink, but she said she would not unless he drank too. The poor man was in a quandary. He hated to break his fast; but he also hated to see the child suffer from thirst. Finally he drank, and the child drank with him.

For a long time he dared not look into the sky, for he feared the star had gone. So imagine his surprise when, on looking up, he saw *two* stars shining brightly above the mountain.

A further story that illustrates the effect of enlightenment

The only thing permanent about our behavior patterns is our belief that they are so.

—MOSHE FELDENKRAIS

describes the devotee who knelt to be initiated into discipleship. The guru whispered the sacred mantra into his ear, warning him not to reveal it to anyone.

"What will happen if I do?" asked the devotee.

Said the guru, "Anyone you reveal the mantra to will be liberated from the bondage of ignorance and suffering, but you yourself will be excluded from discipleship and suffer damnation."

No sooner had he heard those words than the devotee rushed to the marketplace, collected a large crowd around him, and repeated the sacred mantra for all to hear.

The guru's other disciples later reported this to the guru and demanded that the man be expelled for his disobedience.

The guru smiled and said, "He has no need of anything I can teach. His action has shown him to be a guru in his own right."

The difference between knowledge and enlightenment is this: With knowledge, you have a torch that lights the way. With enlightenment, *you* are the torch.

Spiritual masters don't try to change people's lives. They simply point to the insanity, expose the illusions people harbor. When you see, when you become aware, the transformation begins. You don't have to *do* anything. Just look. It may be simple, but it is not easy. Why?

1. Because, as we saw earlier, you are going through life like a drug addict. Imagine that a child is given heroin shots when he or she is first born, and the drug is continued into his or her twenties. Now you tell that person, "Enjoy the sunset, or eat nutritious

We are wide-eyed in contemplating the possibility that life may exist elsewhere in the universe, but we wear blinders when contemplating the possibilities of life on earth.

—DR. NORMAN COUSINS

food." You must be crazy. The only thing this person lives for is the drug! And that's what your life is like—so much denial.

2. Your life is also likened to a hypnotic state.

Many universities invite, each year, hypnotists to enlighten students and teachers regarding the professional advantages of hypnotism. The students rush onstage to be participants. The audience laughs heartily when the students tear at their clothes because it has been suggested to them that the temperature is hot or hug themselves because they think it cold. Why is the audience laughing? Because it is humorous to see someone respond so easily to someone else's suggestion.

I remember the example of an accomplished actress being unable to read the list of nominees for an award at the Academy Awards night. A good friend of hers, Jack Nicholson, practically had to push her out on the stage. She looked terrified. How could so accomplished a woman be affected so strongly? The answer, of course, is that she lived in a tinsel world of her peers, and she was simply paralyzed by it.

3. We are living in a dream world. How can you tell a person that there is another world called "real" when all he or she believes is that this dream is reality?

4. Try to explain to a man or woman born blind the color green. He or she has nothing with which to relate it. Some will offer analogies: "The color green is like soothing music. Or it is like soft velvet." The worst scenario is when they argue, "No, it's music." "No, it's velvet." Next they beat each other over the head

I stopped believing in Santa Claus when my mother took me to see him in a department store, and he asked me for my autograph.

—SHIRLEY TEMPLE

with bats. Neither of them is right, but they fight to defend their positions. Tony used to say, "So somebody finally gets his or her sight, and someone else says, 'Now you know what the color green is!' 'Yes,' she replies, 'I heard it this morning.' " How silly. Even when the reality is before our very eyes, we hang on to our previous beliefs.

What do you have to do to wake up?

First of all, *admit that you are asleep*. Or, to put it another way, that you are not in touch with reality. In one of his "Power Talks," Tony Robbins illustrates this point of phenomenology quite well. He claims that what you are in touch with is not reality but your representation of reality. And all your feelings and emotions are triggered by these representations. An example shows a man holding the door for a woman. One woman says to herself, "Isn't he polite, kind, thoughtful?" Another says, "That male chauvinistic pig. Doesn't he realize that women can open their own doors?"

Can you imagine the emotions that accompany these different representations?

We are convinced we know. Yet our senses constantly betray us.

According to Deepak Chopra, we are sitting still (at least we think we are) yet we are moving at dizzying speeds. We experience the chair (or our bodies) as solid. Yet they are mostly empty space. We filter only a fraction of stimuli that presents itself to us and think that's the total reality. Yet we allow into our consciousness only what we already believe, only what confirms our beliefs. Don't be fooled by that cliché, "Seeing is believing." It's not. We see only what we already believe! Chopra tells of cats raised from birth in rooms that are painted with horizontal stripes and others in rooms that are painted with only vertical stripes. When the kittens grew into adult cats, those raised in the horizontal room bumped into chairs, tables, people. It's not that they didn't see the legs; it's just that their brains had no neural connections that allowed them to recognize vertical objects. The example illustrates superbly how we allow into our brains only what our neural connections permit.

Second, *cultivate the ability to listen*. There is an old saying, "Learn to listen, and listen to learn." Ask yourself: Am I listening to discover something, or only to confirm what I already believe or know?

Tony told the story of a man meeting another man and saying "Henry, you used to be so tall, and now you are so short. You used to be so dark, and now you are so light, you used to be so stout, now you are so thin."

"But I am not Henry," he replied.

"Oh, you've changed your name too!"

We don't have all the answers, yet we won't change our direction when we see where we are going isn't getting us where we want to go. Recently a scientific test was done with rats in a maze. The rats were put there with cheese at the end of the maze. When a rat came up to a blank wall, it would sniff around and then go in another direction. It would keep changing direction till it reached the end of the maze and got the cheese. How different with us humans! When we come to a blank wall, instead of backing off and finding another direction, we just keep hitting our heads against the wall!

Third, *become alert*. You needn't swallow everything you

hear. On the other hand, you don't have to attack it either. Nor do you have to agree with everything you hear. A story is told of a Jesuit superior who was reputed to be the most successful superior we ever had. One day he was asked the secret for his success. He replied, "Easy. I simply agree with everyone, no matter what they say." His interrogator said, "That's stupid. It's crazy. You can't agree with everyone no matter what they say!" The superior answered, "You're right. It is stupid. It *is* crazy to agree with everyone."

The Buddha once said, "O monks and scholars, you must not agree with all that you hear me say. But like a goldsmith, who rubs, scrapes, cuts, and melts, so you must do the same with my words."

There is a connection we should mention between religion and this business of waking up, listening, and staying alert. Religion should prepare you to do these things better, but often it doesn't. Once there was a little boy who came home after dark from his games and worried his mother sick. So she told him that by coming home *after* dark, he had to pass through the forest, and that's when the ghosts or monsters usually came out and could attack him. He was so frightened by this that he would always come home *before* dark.

However, the ruse backfired. One night the mother wanted him to go out to buy milk. He refused on the grounds that he might be attacked by the ghosts in the forest. So the mother, wise and religious woman that she was, gave him a medal of a saint, and said that if he carried this medal, he would be safe. Now the boy went out with *two* fears: one, of the ghosts, and two, that he might lose the medal.

Tony used to say, "Bad religion teaches you to believe in

The best things in life aren't things.

medals. <u>Good religion teaches you there are no ghosts!</u>" On this subject, he also offered this challenging remark: "Be careful you don't inoculate them too early. They may not get the real thing when they get older." So the question now arises: "Okay, I have done my best to be disposed for this 'waking up.' Now what do I do?" When you reflect on the means of waking up, keep this in the back of your mind: <u>To understand things equals learning; to understand others equals wisdom; but to understand yourself, that is enlightenment!</u>

Do you need a great deal of effort to accomplish this? Do you need to leave your business or family and run to a monastery or a mountaintop? Not at all. In fact, talking about effort, all the effort in the world will not get you to sleep if you have insomnia. All the effort in the world will not give you an appetite for a gourmet meal if your stomach is upset. All the compliments you pour out on an individual will not give you genuine admiration for him or her. Effort and strength simply don't work in these cases. Why should they work in the area of spirituality? All the best things in life are free—faith, appetite, love, admiration; that is, they are not subject to human willpower.

Awareness is achieved by one simple human act: self-observation.

And by self-observation I mean the act of watching everything in you and around you as if it were happening to someone else. This watching should be without comment, without attitude, without judgment.

Attachment is the great fabricator of illusions; reality can be attained only by someone who is detached.

—SIMONE WEIL

Not too long ago, Deepak Chopra, whom I have mentioned before, stated an idea that he eventually incorporated in his marvelous book *The Seven Spiritual Laws of Success:* Three things are necessary to achieve what you and I would call an experience of God. He teaches these to all his patients, and they do wonders for their health.

1. *Create silence in your life.* (Remember the mystic who did this for forty years with the result that tigers lay at his feet and snakes wrapped themselves lovingly around his legs. Isn't this the story of the great St. Francis of Assisi, who had a special relation with all animal life?) Silence is created by meditation.

2. *Learn to commune with and be intimate with nature.* Most people love doing this already. To go up a mountain and watch a sunset, to walk by the ocean and listen to the sound of the waves, to wander in a forest and hear the rustle of the leaves and chirping of the birds—what peace and joy this brings to the human heart. Thich Nhat Hanh, a Vietnamese Buddhist monk, in his book *Peace Is Every Step,* even suggests you find a favorite tree and hug it!

3. *Release the need to evaluate, to interpret, to pass moral judgment.*

Never take counsel of your fears.

—General George S. Patton

Tony de Mello would say, "Why eliminate judgment? Because all your moral judgments come from your conditioning anyway!" The reason you prefer the company of certain people and avoid others is that you have been carefully educated to like and dislike.

This self-observation is also called passive detachment. When things happen in your life—for example, a negative experience such as rejection or depression—don't try to change it. Observe it, understand it. Don't personalize it, saying "I am depressed," "I am rejected." Be like the sky observing these clouds coming in and going out of your life. You are not your depression or your rejection, any more than you are your job, career, name, fame, or even your body ("I'm fat, I'm balding, I'm beautiful," etc.).

Here is an example of self-observation.

Imagine you are the father or mother of a little child whom you love dearly. But you know he is only a child and is having a crying tantrum. He's not getting his way with something and he has his cute little face screwed up in that angry, hurt, crying pose that is so amusing that you have to smile at it. "Oh, it's okay. He's living in his own little child's world." But what he is demanding is simply not good for him, and you wisely don't give in to his tantrum. Even when he flails away at you with his tiny fists, you just hold his head at a distance so you won't be hurt and let him swing away. Years later when you describe this incident to him, now that he is an adult, he is bound to say, "Did I do that? Oh, well, I was a child and living in another world, wasn't I?"

What I like about this analogy to awakening is that when

people criticize you, when you are treated unfairly, just look on them as you would at that little child. You can really love them because you recognize they are living in an insane world where completely different values and priorities have been drummed into them by their programming and conditioning. Don't you get caught up in their little world, their insanity!

The sad part is that they don't want to get out of that world with all its insanity. They use Band-Aids to heal their hurts. They do not want a cure, they want relief. This is what true spirituality leads *you* to. It puts you in an adult world while all the rest of humankind are playing in the kindergarten playpen with their toys of big business, government, show business. Spirituality wakes you up and gets you out of that childish world into an adult world where paradoxically you can let the child within you come forth freely. It wasn't for nothing that Jesus, the greatest spiritual master of all, once said, "Unless you become as little children, you shall not enter the kingdom of heaven."

One of the most precious gifts of spirituality (or "waking up") is freedom. First, freedom to be all that you are and can be. Second, freedom from fear. Fear of failure, of rejection, of death. Now religion should do all this for you. Religion is like a finger pointing to the moon, but foolishly we grasp or put our arms around the trappings of religion, ritual, dogma, and forget all about in which direction it is pointing us to go.

In the East it is said, "Where the finger is pointing to the moon, all that the fool sees is the finger." And Jean Guitton, the philosopher, vividly adds, "And then uses that finger to pluck out his eye!"

I recall the first time Tony was interviewed on commercial television. He was asked by the interviewer, Dorothy Farley, why he was so popular, why so many people wanted to hear him. His reply went something like this: "I think people are fed up with God-talk. What they want and need is an experience of God in their lives. They hear so many words, words, words. It's like going into a restaurant and looking at the menu all night and never getting around to the wonderful meal. Even worse, it's like eating the menu!"

If a significant person in your life offends you, you ought to be angered. If you are not appreciated for the good work you do, it is only normal (so they say) that you should be hurt and feel depressed. If your best friend turns his or her back on you and walks out of your life—or worse, into the arms of another (especially someone you can't stand)—you must feel rejected, lonely, even worthless.

Spirituality teaches you that all these so-called normal, natural reactions are not truly natural, but induced, imposed, taught, and learned. Spirituality says there is a better, sounder way of living.

Realize first that this crazy, insane kind of existence doesn't have to continue. Like any addiction, you have been drugged from your earliest days.

Second, realize that no matter how much we protest that we want to get out of this insanity, we really don't. We have been hypnotized into thinking "It's all right, things will improve." It's like becoming the CEO of Ward C in a state hospital, a place for the mentally unstable.

I remember my father, who was a supervisor at Brooklyn State Hospital, introduced me to patients who thought they were building rockets and space crafts for *Star Wars* and were

The mind is its own place, and in itself can make heaven of Hell, or a hell of Heaven.

—JOHN MILTON

all worried that their inventions were not coming out right. When I asked him why he indulged them in their fantasies, he simply replied, "It's all right. They are living in another world."

Third, develop the ability to listen. There's a story about Nasruddin (more about him later), who played only one note on his musical instrument. His disciples were going crazy listening to him as he strummed only his single note. In exasperation they complained, "Mullah, why don't you vary your tune?" He replied scornfully, "Those others are still searching for the right note. I have found it." And he went on strumming his one note.

It is only when you create silence in your life that you can listen, only when you admit you don't know that you become open to the revelation of God in everything. God is in his creation as the voice of the singer is in his song. How can you listen to the song and not recognize the singer? How can you watch a dance and not see the dancer? Sometimes we are like the man who when he hears that someone is enraptured by the beauty of the sunset goes off looking for the "beauty." He doesn't realize that "beauty" isn't a thing. It's a way of seeing.

An exquisite story illustrates listening. In fact, it is the finest story that Tony ever told. There was a temple built on an island with large, medium, and small bells crafted by the finest bell makers in the world. When the winds blew, the bells would peal in a symphony that would enrapture the heart of the hearer, sending him into ecstasy. Eventually the island sank into the sea and with it the temple and its bells.

But a legend persisted that if you listen attentively, you could still hear the bells peal. And the heart of the hearer

Concentrate on silence. When it comes, dwell on what it sounds like. Then strive to carry that quiet wherever you go.

—PAUL WILSON, *THE LITTLE BOOK OF CALM*

would be filled with ecstasy. A young man traveled thousands of miles to test for himself the validity of this legend. He sat down on the sand opposite where the island had sunk into the sea and listened intently to hear the bells. However, all he could hear was the sound of the waves crashing against the shore.

After several weeks of fruitless effort he went up to the town and heard the pundits tell that the legend was true and that those who heard the bells would be enraptured. Inflamed by these stories, he returned to his place on the sand and listened again even more intently to hear the bells. However, all he heard was more waves crashing against the shore. After several weeks of no success he said to himself, "Perhaps I am not destined to hear the bells, or perhaps the legend is not true." So he decided to go home, abandoning his project. After he packed his bags, he decided once more to visit the spot where he could say good-bye to the sand, the coconut trees, the sky. As he lay on the sand, he heard the sound of the waves crashing as they always did on the shore. This time he did not try to push the sound away. But as he listened to the sound of the waves, it created a silence within him so deep that he became barely conscious of himself.

And it was in the depth of that silence that he heard the first tinkle of a bell, then another and another, until he heard a full symphony of bells. And his heart was enraptured and soared into ecstasy.

Tony's comment: If you want to hear the bells, listen to the sound of the sea.

This is not a telephone-answering machine,
but a questioning machine. Who are you, and
what do you want? If you think these are trivial
questions, be aware that most people come into
this world and leave it without answering
either one!

—JOAN BORYSENKO

study

1. *Admit we are asleep.* We are not in touch with reality. It is difficult to recognize this fact because we have been programmed to believe our dream state is real. How do you explain light to a person born blind, who knows only darkness? All our experience is by contrast: pleasure, pain, light, dark, certainty, doubt.
2. *Become able to listen.* Are we really trying to find out, to discover, or are we trying to confirm what we already know?
3. *Stay alert, without judging.* Become aware of everything, inside you and outside you, without comment, without attitude, without judgment.

Postscript: If you wish to broaden your study of meditation, I highly recommend the tapes of Jack Kornfield. His series, called *The Inner Art of Meditation,* published by Nightingale-Conant, is excellent. Tony de Mello provided an opportunity for all the students of his institute in India to make a Vipassana retreat. Kornfield explains this method of meditation and gives exercises to practice it.

May your joys be as deep as the ocean, and your sorrows as light as its foam.

—W. N. CLARKE, S.J.

two

Happiness

It is easy to say that happiness as a principle of spirituality concerns everyone in his or her pursuit of life goals. It is the object of everyone's search. Happiness, success, joy, peace, serenity. The question we all have is how to attain these.

St. Augustine once said, "Thou hast made us for Thyself, O Lord, and our hearts will not rest, till they rest in Thee." Why have those words become the favorite of many millions, repeated for centuries?

Stories abound. Consider the one about the rabbi who is faithful for so many years to his synagogue duties. One day he asks God for a favor. "God, you know how faithful I have

Every time you think you are not happy, say "I am happy." Say it strongly to yourself, even if your feelings are contradictory. Remember, it is your self-image and not you. Just as fast as a fish can move in water, you can instantly change to a happy, balanced attitude.

—T. Tulku Rinpoche

been these past seventy years, how devoted my wife has been. Now I have a favor to ask of you. Let me win the lottery!"

A few weeks go by, but nothing happens. A few months . . . nothing! More months, and when nothing happens, the rabbi goes to the altar of the synagogue, crying out "God, give me a break!" God answers, "Give me a break yourself. *Buy a ticket!*"

If you search the Sacred Scriptures, you will find statements such as "All creation is shot through with joy!" How come we don't experience it?

Kabir, the Eastern poet, would say, "I laughed when they told me the fish in the water was thirsty." Only the human fish is thirsty.

Why the story and the sayings strike a responsive chord in your heart is because happiness is not something you need to strive for. You already have it.

You don't have to do anything to make the sun rise. Just open the shutters on the window; let the brightness and the warmth in.

Again, to illustrate this point, you hear stories about the small fish and the big fish. A little fish swims up to the big fish and says, "You're much bigger than me; much more intelligent and experienced. Can you tell me where the ocean is?" The big fish looks at him and says, "The ocean? Why, it's all around you. You are swimming in it." The little fish scornfully looks at him and says, "Don't be silly. This is just water," and swims away looking for the ocean.

In India they tell the following story of Nasruddin, who apparently is the butt of many jokes. Nasruddin is on his knees in front of his cottage searching for something in the grass. His disciples come along, see him in this inglorious posture, and ask,

Every belief is a limit to be examined and transcended.

—JOHN C. LILLY

"Mullah, have you lost something?" He replies, "Yes, I have lost the key to my cottage!" So down go all the disciples on their knees and help Nasruddin in his search. After about fifteen minutes of fruitless looking, one disciple asks him, "Mullah, do you have any idea where you might have lost the key?" "Of course," replies Nasruddin. "I lost it in the house!" "Then why in heaven's name are we looking for it out here?" "Because," says Nasruddin, "there is much more light with which to see!"

There was a famous story about a Scotsman named McGregor who had a recurring dream that if he went south to London Bridge, he would find there a treasure that would solve his money worries forever. Finally he got up the courage to follow his dream and traveled the many miles to London. When he got to London Bridge, he saw it was heavily guarded by the famous Beefeater Guards, so he was hesitant to start looking for his treasure. The head of the guards, seeing him walking near the bridge for several days, came over and questioned him. McGregor thought the guard was a kindly person, so he revealed his dream. The guard laughed and said, "Do you mean to tell me, you believe in dreams? Why, if I followed a dream I have frequently, you'd see how foolish I would be. I have a dream to go north to Scotland, find the house of a man named McGregor, and look under his stovepipe, where I will find a treasure."

McGregor's eyes widened as the guard told the story. He turned on his heels, ran back to his house in Scotland, looked under his stovepipe, and found his treasure.

If happiness is uncaused, if it is surrounding us, if we already have it, then why do we not experience it?

There is a brilliant saying in the East: "When the eye is unobstructed, the result is sight; when the ear is unobstructed, the result is hearing; when the mind is unobstructed, the result is wisdom; and of course when the heart is unobstructed, the result is love."

The reason we don't experience the happiness we already possess is that *we* block it out. Those shutters, which I referred to in the sun analogy, are the myths and illusions we harbor. And once our minds fixate on them, it is almost impossible to dislodge them.

I recall a story told by Archbishop Lawrence Burke, S.J., then the archbishop of the Bahamas. In the hospital he was put in a bed next to an Irishman. Archbishop Burke, despite his Irish-sounding name, is Jamaican, and black. When the priest came the next day to give communion to the patients, he looked on the list and saw "Bishop Burke." Certainly this black man could not be a bishop or named Burke. So he gave communion to the Irishman in the next bed. Archbishop Burke thought it an honest mistake, but when the nun came around the next day to give communion and did the same thing, he decided to do something about it. To his credit, the archbishop told this story without rancor or blame, but simply to make a point: how easy it is to get ideas fixed in the mind and how difficult it is to dislodge them.

To experience the happiness that is ours, we must learn the painful art of dropping illusions. It's painful because they have taken such deep root in our psyches that to tear away the tentacles is like tearing yourself inside out. This art of dropping illusions is difficult because there is such denial. Wherever there is a deep-rooted addiction, you will find denial. When faced with the damage they are doing to their families, businesses, and personal lives, alcoholics or drug addicts can look you straight in the eye and say, "I don't have a problem!"

How do you tell people caught up in a dream that there is another world called reality, when all they can conceive is that their dream is reality? How do you explain to a man born blind, who sits in darkness all day, the experience of light? You don't sweep out darkness with a broom (i.e., by discussing it or forming a committee to study it). You light a candle or turn on the switch. Behold, the darkness vanishes.

ILLUSIONS

Lighting a candle or turning a switch means simply to focus on and reveal the illusion. The first step is to understand that what you're looking at is an illusion. Let us look at just a few illusions. Remove these illusions from your life and you will experience enormous happiness.

Illusion #1. "I will experience success, joy, happiness if I can control or change the external things in my life."

For example, if I can change my boss at work or the location of my business, if everyone I encounter—my subordinates, associates, business partners—agrees with all that I do. If I can change my neighborhood, my spouse, and so on.

The underlying belief here, which has subconsciously entered and dominated your thinking, is that success equals control of external things, people, money, deals. You can no more experience success in work or happiness in life by controlling external things than you can improve your mind by changing

Leave it to others to be perfect, to be wonderful. Be content with what you are—you'll be much more relaxed as a result.

—PAUL WILSON, *THE LITTLE BOOK OF CALM*

your hat or improve your handwriting by changing your pen. All your energy and resources are spent on controlling these externals. It's like paving the entire road of life so that the pebbles and stones don't hurt your bare feet. You can do that, of course, but it will take all your time, energy, resources. Better just to go out and buy a good pair of walking shoes.

Illusion #2. "It's important to be loved, important, respected, well thought of."

To be loved? Human beings are born with two natural urges: to love and to be free. Put all your attention on thinking well of others and not seeking their approval, affection, and love, and you will see a marked difference in your life.

To be important? When I was a young boy, again my father took me to his place of business—Brooklyn State Hospital. Looking through one of the corridor windows, I could see a patient with a papier-mâché king's crown on his head. He was sitting on a chair, which he had convinced the other patients was his throne, and also convinced them that if they came and kissed his hand, he would bestow on them special privileges. I was shocked when the other patients lined up, giggling, and did exactly that!

Tony de Mello used to say we are living in a worldwide insane asylum. "I am the CEO. The chairman of the department. Come kiss my hand and you will receive special favors!" Isn't this a parable of our lives?

Illusion #3. "If all my desires are fulfilled, then I will be happy."

Do you know the story of the woman who was always asking

Nothing in all creation is so like God as stillness.

—MEISTER ECKHART

God for favors? Finally God says, "I've had enough. I am going to grant you any three requests, but after that, no more!" Excitedly she says, "Any three things I want?" "Any three things," says God. She says, "Well, I'm a little embarrassed to ask this, but my husband is a pain in the neck. I'd like to get rid of him." "Granted," says God.

At her husband's wake, all her friends come to sympathize at her loss and say, "How sad. I remember how courteous he was to you. The way he would hold the chair for you at a table in a restaurant. He was so good and kind to you." When she heard all these nice things, she regretted her decision and said to God, "I want him back!" "Granted," says God. Several months go by, and God says to her, "You still have another request coming. What would you like?" She says, "I'm all confused. Some friends say, 'Ask for a million dollars.' Others say, 'What good is a lot of money if you don't have your health? Ask for perfect health.' So I am all confused. Wait a minute. You're pretty wise. What do you suggest I should ask for?" God throws his head back and laughs. "Okay, I'll tell you what you should ask for. Ask to be content with whatever you get!"

Illusion #4. "Thrills and excitement bring true happiness."

Suppose you give a racing stallion a load of sugar, which he may find very tasty to eat. But he is not going to win many races with that diet. What he needs are oats and good nutritious feed. Some people say, "What else is life for, if not to enjoy thrills and excitement?" The wise person answers, "Abiding contentment."

Nothing real can be threatened. Nothing unreal exists.

—MARIANNE WILLIAMSON, QUOTING FROM
THE COURSE IN MIRACLES

Illusion #5. "I believe someone else can do it for me."

"A guru? I must find him!" You are your own guru. You don't need to search further than yourself.

Illusion #6. "I believe that events, circumstances, persons have the power to make me happy (or unhappy)."

They don't. The only power they have is the power you give them.

HOW TO EXPERIENCE HAPPINESS

Here are some suggestions to help you experience God or the happiness you already possess.

1. Develop an attitude of gratitude.

You cannot be truly grateful and unhappy at the same time. They just don't go together. They are incompatible. Ask yourself, "What would happen if I let go?"

In his book *The Seven Spiritual Laws of Success,* Deepak Chopra suggests several ways to experience God (or happiness) in your life. First, create silence. This doesn't mean to live in a mental vacuum, but to become aware of the present moment. This is where you are—always. Most of us live too much in the past, which is unreal—the past is over, gone—or too much in the future, which is also unreal, because it hasn't come yet. Tony used to say, "A neurotic is someone who worries about things in the past that never happened. Not like us normal people who only worry about things in the future that won't happen!"

The Universe is change; our life is what our thoughts make it.

—MARCUS AURELIUS ANTONINUS

God (or if you have another name for God, use it) is the God of the "real," not the "unreal." Most of us allow past problems or future concerns to dominate our present moments. The result is anxiety, frustration, depression, hopelessness.

Tony told the story of the man being chased by a ferocious lion. He comes to a cliff and jumps off into a chasm thousands of feet below. The man grabs a branch sticking out from the cliff side, looks up, sees the hungry lion above, looks down, and sees the yawning chasm below. Then he notices on the branch a red berry. He plucks it, puts it in his mouth, eats it, and says, "How sweet it is!" Now, that's living in the present!

You can use the past and learn from it. You can use the future and plan for it. That's good. Just don't *live* in either.

2. Be intimate with nature.

You have heard it said by spiritual masters, "Watch the grass grow." "Hug a tree." "Smell the flowers." I am convinced that artists, those who are so sensitive to nature, who see things in nature that I or others like me don't normally see, are close to becoming mystics.

3. Live a life of nonjudgment. (This is the most difficult of all the precepts.)

How can we go through life without making judgments? Don't I say, "This is good, I'll buy it. This is bad, I'll avoid it"? These judgments are okay. It's the *moral* judgments that we make so easily that we must drop: "He's dumb!" "She's guilty!" "She's really a self-centered person!" How do we know?

As Tony Robbins suggests, the way to live this life of nonjudgment is by being a perceiver, not a judger. Try to deter-

You have no idea what a poor opinion I have of myself—and how little I deserve it.

—W. S. GILBERT

mine what this person, this event is trying to teach you. Perhaps someone at work says something that really offends you. Your emotional reaction may be anger or perhaps hurt, even violence. Or you can ask yourself, "What is this person teaching me?" It might be compassion. You may find yourself saying "What an awful thing it must be to work at a job you don't like!" The result of these efforts: Frustration evaporates, impatience diminishes, joy and happiness in life increase.

4. Control the focus of your attention.

I was working in a parish in the Bahamas preparing a homily for the New Year's midnight Mass. Two armed robbers appeared at my door. When they didn't get much satisfaction about the money they wanted to steal, one of the robbers told the other to put the rifle on me. I was quite concerned that I might be shot, so I grabbed the barrel of the gun and pointed it away from me. In pulling the gun away, the robber shot a hole in the ceiling. Afterward, they fled.

Later I was referred to as "the Rambo priest." I have had a lot of fun telling that story, but at the time it was frightening and could have been tragic. Making an amusing story of it was my way to control the focus, to prevent the event from having lasting traumatic effects.

5. Surround yourself with happy people.

In Tony Robbins's words: "The purpose of life is to be happy. This is success. Not to be happy is failure."

three

Self

Earlier I mentioned that the emphasis of this book is on you as a treasure. Not only you as an individual, but as a group of hundreds, thousands, perhaps even millions reading these words. When I imagine who you are, I am astounded at the variety. Businessmen and women at workplaces, religious, priests, lay folk, and you who are the backbone of our society—creators and keepers of our families. What a group! I feel privileged to say this to you. You really are a treasure.

Yet, despite the fact that you have this great potential, so many things militate against your experiencing yourselves as great: your culture, education, family upbringing ("no prophet is recognized . . ."), even at times your religious training (which can be a very strong conditioner). It has been said of religion, "If you inoculate them with religion too young, they might not get the real thing when they are older!"

Discovering who you are is the most important spiritual discovery you can make. Questions such as "Who is God? Who is Jesus?" are very important, but most important is the question "Who am I?"

Some years ago a young pretty co-ed at a university threw her arms about my neck and said so warmly, "Father Stroud, I love you. You remind me so much of . . . [in my fantasy I immediately supplied Robert Redford, Cary Grant] you remind me so much of *my grandfather!*" I instantly sent her packing. How easily we think we are someone else.

The way this theme is expressed in spiritual literature is "the loss of self." It is a theme that recurs: "Unless a grain of wheat fall into the ground and die . . ." or "You must die to your very self if you wish to be my disciple. . . ." To call this theme the "loss of self" is perhaps a misnomer. It would be better to call it "finding one's self," because what you are asked to die to is the false self, even the false "selves" we have created. We tend to identify with our careers, our fame, our name, and because we do, we lose sight of our true and beautiful selves. From a spiritual viewpoint, therefore, the principle is very positive.

You can't find a more apt image of this principle than the one from the Scriptures. You are like a seed. A seed has so much potential for growth and beauty. However, it has a hard protective shell surrounding it. When springtime comes, the hard shell has to go, or the flower will not appear. If the shell doesn't die, the protector becomes the destroyer.

Most people live . . . in a very restricted circle of their potential being. They make use of a very small portion of their possible consciousness . . . much like a man who, out of his whole bodily organism, should get into using and moving only his little finger.

Our ego resembles that hard shell. When we are young, we need that protection. Others have to feed us, cuddle us, and love us. Our fragile beings cannot withstand abuse; we need protection. So we develop what in psychological terms is called "primary ego defenses." As noted earlier, we find that as little boys if we push back our antagonists, they give in, and we gain the reputation of being a bully. Or if we are little girls and play the "coquette" with our grandparents, we can get whatever we want. These are effective defenses and work well for us. However, when it is time for them to go, the hard shell of these defenses complains, "But I have been so good to you. Don't let me die." Nevertheless, if we don't, we will never grow to our true potential. "I must let you go. If I don't, the protector becomes the destroyer."

A story to communicate what happens when we *don't* let go tells of an eaglet. One day a farmer found an eagle's egg. So he put it in with the eggs of the barnyard chickens. All the eggs hatched together, so when the eaglet saw the chicks scrape their little claws on the ground, it scraped its little claw on the ground. When it heard them "cluck, cluck," it clucked also. When it saw them flap their wings and jump up on a branch, it did the same. It simply thought it was a little chicken.

One day when the eaglet was much older, it looked up in the sky and saw a magnificent bird with its wings outstretched, majestically flying up and down the currents of air. It turned to one of the chickens and asked, "Who is that?" The chicken replied, "Oh, that's the golden eagle, the king of all the birds. But don't you give another thought to it. We are just little chickens." And the sad ending of the story is that the eagle

Intelligence is much greater than intellect, for it is the integration of reason and love. But there can be intelligence only when there is self-knowledge, the deep understanding of the total process of oneself.

—J. KRISHNAMURTI

went to its death, never realizing that it too was a golden eagle. Till its dying day it continued to think that it was nothing but a little chicken.

In India hunters have a simple but effective way to capture monkeys. They cut a hole in a coconut large enough for a monkey's hand to go in, but small enough to hold it captive if it makes a fist. They then put a banana into the coconut and wire the coconut to a tree. The monkey puts its hand into the coconut, grabs the banana, but cannot get its hand out because it won't open its fist and let the banana go.

FALSE SELVES

In the same way, once we identify with these false selves, we become like those poor monkeys. We refuse to let go of these false identities. Freedom and joy will come if only we let go, but we will not!

Here is another interesting scenario. You are a counselor, an advisor. In comes a man dressed in a three-cornered hat and military jacket of a nineteenth-century French general. You ask him his name. He says, "I am General Bonaparte." You say, "Not Napoleon Bonaparte?" "Yes," he says, "the very same." You think to yourself, "I better go along with him. He may be dangerous." So you say aloud, "Well, General, how can I help you?" He has a very determined but worried look in his eyes. "I am concerned because tomorrow I go into battle with the Duke of Wellington at Waterloo. I can't sleep at night because I don't know whether to deploy my troops around his flanks or to attack him directly up the middle.

All that we are is the result of what we have thought.

—BUDDHA

What would you advise?" Now, if you were to reply, "I have studied these battle schemes extensively, and think the best route to follow is . . ." you should be put into the crazy house with the poor fellow who thinks he is Napoleon.

If you really want to help him, you must pull the rug out (so to speak) from underneath him. You must somehow show him that he is not Napoleon. Once he is convinced of that, where do all those worries about the battle go? They become nonexistent.

The question put to yourself then arises: How do we develop these false selves? Answer: By a process of identification. Identification is the means by which we emotionally and mentally lose ourselves in something inside or outside of us. For example, you identify with the shape of your body. You say, "I am fat. I am balding. I am aging. I am beautiful." Or you identify with your name. If it appears in headlines, you are elated. When it does not show up on the awards list or the honor roll, you are disappointed, depressed. You identify with your fame, what others think of you, your image, your reputation. That is when you develop a false self.

Remember, no one accepts *you* or rejects *you,* only their image of you. They are conditioned to like this or that, so why should you be happy or sad because of what others think or say? In the film *The Gods Must Be Crazy,* the African native has a completely different reaction than I do to the beautiful white woman who is on the safari. He is conditioned to find attractive a woman whose hair is short and kinky, whose neck has been elongated from birth, whose ears have huge rings in the lobes. So when he describes to his fellow tribesmen this "ugly white woman, with long stringy yellow hair, short neck,

As a man thinketh, so is he, and as a man chooseth, so is he and so is nature.

—Ralph Waldo Emerson

unadorned ear lobes," as a westerner, I am appalled at his lack of perception of beauty. From my point of view, she is a lovely actress carefully chosen by Hollywood agents for the part.

Now push the scenario further. Suppose you find the woman weeping, and you ask her why, and she tells you that she is depressed because the man refuses to marry her, finding her unattractive. You would try to convince her that he simply has been educated differently by his upbringing, by his culture, to find other types of women attractive. "You must be crazy to respond to his reaction with these tears!"

As Tony de Mello used to say (to the consternation of many of his listeners), "Don't get excited if someone tells you he or she loves you. You are only fitting his or her shopping list!"

In fact, you have been conditioned to evaluate even yourself. Ask yourself, "What is *my* conditioned criterion for evaluating myself?"

A further identity crisis develops when you identify with your profession: "I am a lawyer." "I am a bishop." "I am a CEO." Even "I am a failed businessman." Someone set you up for this. You are *not* your job, your rank, your profession. These are mere costumes you wear.

A group of children are all dressed in their costumes ready to go on stage for the ballet. Several children run up to the stage manager just before the curtain is about to go up and say, "Where are the toilets?" The manager looks at them and asks, "Are you boys or girls?" The children answer, "Neither. We're little squirrels!" Children can be expected to identify with their roles, but not adults!

Can you imagine an actress winning an Academy Award for playing the part of a prostitute (as Jane Fonda did in *Klute)* and then becoming a prostitute, thinking "Well, if they thought I was so great playing the role of a prostitute, I might as well be one!" You would say she is crazy. It was only a role, a costume she wore for a film. You don't translate that into real life!

So identification means wrongly to take something as being part of your essential self. Enjoy your name, your career, your fame, your good looks, but don't identify with them. You must learn the art of enjoying life, enjoying all these things that make up life. And you can enjoy them only when you don't fear change or loss. Enjoy things because they are impermanent. So many of us have lost the capacity for enjoyment. For example, in music if we tell the orchestra leader to "hold that note" or "keep playing that chord, I like it," we will never hear the symphony.

How then do you "lose" your false self or selves? Have you ever tried to lose anything deliberately? Try it. You will find it impossible. Can you lose something by renunciation? No. What you renounce, you are forever tied to. Tony used to say, "Whenever prostitutes come to me, they want to talk about God. Priests come, they want to talk about sex!" It's what these people have renounced that enthralls them.

In *Taking Flight,* Tony also tells the fine story of the woodcarver. When the Duke of Lu sees the carver's magnificent bell frames, he remarks, "What sort of genius can make these beautiful bell frames?" The woodcarver replies, "I am no genius, but what I do before actually carving out the bell frame is to meditate for three days to calm my mind. After three days of meditating, I no longer think of rewards or emoluments. After five days, I no longer think of praise or blame, skill or awkwardness. After seven days, I lose all sense of my limbs, my body, my very self. I lose all consciousness of my surroundings, the court. Only my skill remains. It is in this state that I go into the forest and find the tree that holds the bell frame I envision. My hands go to work driven by my spirit. Perhaps this is why people say my work is the work of spirits."

Some time ago, I heard the marvelous Itzhak Perlman play the violin in the Hollywood Bowl. He was so far away I could hardly see him. However, a year later, he was playing at Lincoln Center. It was televised live and of course you could see him close up. During the intermission a taped interview he had with a group of wide-eyed young students from the famous Juilliard School of Music was played. The students' question to him was "How do we become like you?"

I will never forget his answer. He replied, "There are three things. One, God has given me this great talent. Two, I have this beautiful musical instrument, the Stradivarius violin. Three, I have the magnificent music of Beethoven (or others). I try to put them all together and get out of the way!"

When the program resumed, I looked at his face while he played. His eyes were closed. He seemed like he was somewhere else. He seemed to be in ecstasy. (The word "ecstasy" comes from the Greek, *ek* = outside, and *stateo* = to stand, to stand outside oneself.) So being happy is one sure way of losing yourself. When you see an enjoyable film, when you are engrossed in an engaging novel, you are said to "lose" yourself in the fine experience. You are never so conscious of your "self" as when you are in pain: headaches, toothaches, ego-

*I am larger, better than I thought. I did not
know I held such goodness.*

—WALT WHITMAN

aches. You are never so beside yourself as when you are happy. Perlman was "ecstatic" ("standing outside" himself).

How then do you deal with these "identity crises" when you become aware of them? When you experience this lack of happiness, this negativity?

One way is to depersonalize the negative feeling. Avoid saying to yourself, "I am sad. I am nervous. I am depressed." Better to say "There is sadness in my life. I am experiencing a depression in my life." You are like the sky. The sadness and depression are clouds that you look at from your place above. By detaching the false sense of identity, you also detach the distress it creates.

When the Buddha was asked what it was like to be enlightened, he replied, "Before enlightenment, I was depressed. After enlightenment, I continue to be depressed!" (But with a difference—he did not identify with his depression!)

If you learn to do this, what will be the result? Fish in the water do not get wet! They thrive on it. Real people in life don't get hurt. They thrive on everything that happens to them.

Nothing (no-thing), no person, no event or circumstance has the power to hurt you. The only power it has is what you give it. Refuse to hand over such power.

Life is a symphony. In the symphony of life, you don't care whether you are the flutist or the drummer. You enjoy the music, the march of the band. There is no need to lead. The inner self is quite content to be the trumpeter, the flutist, even part of the audience. It's the drugged ego that insists on being the drum major or the orchestra leader.

Life is too vital for concern over being rich or poor, fa-

I have been through some terrible things in my life, some of which actually happened.

—MARK TWAIN

mous or unknown, fat or thin, popular or ignored, handsome or plain. We spend our energies on so many useless pursuits. And as soon as you have the things you want, they become colorless, like pebbles surrounding a sparkling diamond. It's like using a precious manuscript to light a fire, a thousand-dollar bill to light a cigar!

You are a treasure. Who you really are, your true self, is magnificent. That is why you must set about finding it. And that is what spirituality is all about: finding out who you truly are.

All suffering prepares the soul for vision.

—MARTIN BUBER

four

Suffering and Illusion

Most of us would like to eliminate suffering from our lives. Although you may not or cannot eliminate it fully, the great spiritual teachers point to ways you can rid yourselves of most of it. We should say at the start, however, that you have to distinguish between suffering and pain. The two are not the same. We can endure pain and still maintain happiness. For example, mountain climbers, attempting to reach the peak, endure cuts and bruises that they don't even notice in their quest to conquer the summit. Their hearts are filled with the exhilaration of the climb. Football players act similarly. How many pictures have you seen of players sitting on the bench, hands and arms covered with mud, grime, bloody injuries, and yet their minds and hearts are focused on the outcome of the game?

Whatever one believes to be true either is true or becomes true in one's mind.

—JOHN C. LILLY

Even in going to a dentist, we will submit to the pain involved provided we see a happy ending: good, healthy teeth.

One graphic example I recall involves the Los Angeles Dodgers, who were near to winning the World Series in 1988. The player who stood out in the race to the pennant was Kirk Gibson. But he was so beaten up at the beginning of the World Series that Tommy Lasorda, the Dodger manager, decided to let him rest for the first game. However, the game went to the ninth inning with the score tied and two outs. Lasorda was forced to call on Gibson to pinch hit. Gibson could hardly walk, his knees and arms bothered him so. But he stood up and hit a home run to win the game. Watching Gibson run around the bases was really amazing. Although he was in severe pain, he put his fist in a thumbs-up victory gesture and had a big smile on his face. There it was: no incompatibility between pain and happiness.

But suffering is a horse of a different color. In suffering, your imaginary picture of how things should be, or the way you want them to be, clashes with what actually happens. It's desire clashing with reality.

Suppose you want to be appreciated for your work, be promoted. What happens? The usual. Someone else is promoted. You are passed over. You want to have a deep relationship with a friend, but he or she walks out of your life. Even worse, into the arms of someone you can't stand!

The Buddha once said, "The world is full of sorrow. The root of sorrow is desire. The uprooting of sorrow is desirelessness." Of course, desires in themselves are good. They are energy. You wouldn't be reading this book if you didn't *desire* to profit from it for yourself. But when your happiness depends

*If you want the rainbow, you have to put up
with the rain. At the end of a life without
adversity, it is hard to find a rainbow.*

—DOLLY PARTON

on the fulfillment of that desire, you have an "attachment." And *that* was what the Buddha was referring to.

Here is another way of putting it: In his book *Song of the Bird,* Tony de Mello tells a story from ancient India that I call the "good luck, bad luck" story. A man has two great loves in his life. One is his son, and the other is a beautiful stallion. His servants come in one day and say, "Bad luck. That stallion you love so well just ran away." So the man goes into deep depression over his loss. The next day the servants come and say, "Good luck. That stallion that ran away yesterday returned today bringing with him three beautiful wild mares." Now the man who had been so depressed is elated. The next day the servants return and say, "Bad luck. Your son, whom you love so well, was trying to break in one of the new horses but fell and broke his leg." So, the man goes from the heights of ecstasy to the depths of depression again. The next day the servants say, "Good luck. The army that is fighting this crazy war, conscripting every able-bodied young man, when they saw your son and his broken leg refused to take him." So up again go the father's emotions.

As you can see, there is no end to this story. One day the man is up, the next day he is down. Because he has allowed his happiness to depend on things external to himself, he is living in what Deepak Chopra refers to as the "object referral" mode. True happiness, however, can be experienced only by living in the "self-referral" mode.

It is hard for us to believe, but what we fail to realize is that we resist so much the natural state of happiness that should be ours. Consider the man submerged up to his neck in a vat of liquid excrement. He doesn't ask to be taken out of the vat. He just says, "Please don't make any waves!"

You can suffer from suffering or you can dissolve it by understanding its true nature. Suffering is a face-to-face encounter with something you don't want to face. It's your resistance against truth. Against reality. Against the very truth that would liberate you if you would only face it.

Suffering is nature's attempt to help us face illusions we don't even suspect we harbor.

We are so conditioned, so programmed; we walk through life with assumptions we never challenge. Like the two hunters who flew into the jungle to hunt rhinoceros. They told the pilot to come back in a week to pick them up. When the pilot returned, the hunters had bagged two large rhinos. The pilot said, "We can't take them in the plane. They're too heavy." The hunters said, "Why not? The last pilot we had took them." The pilot said, "He did? Okay, pile them in."

So off they went, but they were not in the air five minutes before they crashed. As the hunters crawled out from the wreckage, one of them said to the other, "Where do you think we are?" "About fifty feet," replied the other, "from where we crashed the last time."

Assumptions, assumptions, assumptions. Hidden, and never challenged.

George Bernard Shaw used to say, "[Suffering or] heartbreak is life educating us."

It's how we react to suffering that makes the difference. As Tony said: "Some people take refuge in self-pity. Some take refuge in high-sounding rationalizations. Some try to escape suffering in activity. All give the ghost an existence it does not have, apart from your illusions, no matter what form it takes—loneliness, frustration, despair."

You can deal with suffering if you understand it. Most people deal with it the way they deal with a car that is broken down. They kick it, shout at it, walk away from it, pretend nothing is wrong with it. All you need do is lift the hood, see what the failure is (perhaps a dead spark plug), and repair it. Face the inner breakdown and correct it.

Most people claim they want a cure, but what they really want is a painkiller. They want relief from the pressure: "Give me back my health, my good looks, my youth."

They don't really want to escape the kindergarten of life, the baby playpen. All they want is someone to repair their broken toys.

We run to gurus, to psychologists, when in reality we have it all if we learn to live in this self-referral mode.

Tony, a psychologist himself, knew the value of psychology, so with tongue in cheek he would tell this story about a boy in a school for retarded children. (He was not so retarded, as will soon be clear.) The teacher had given all the children in the class the assignment to make something out of the clay she had distributed. When she approached Johnny, she said, "Hi, Johnny." He said, "Hi." She asked, "What are you playing with, Johnny?"

He replied, "Horse manure." ("Ugh," she thought.) "What are you making of your . . . horse manure?" "A teacher!" he said. She thought she better report this to the principal, so she told the principal, "I think Johnny has regressed. Maybe you better speak to him." The principal said, "Hi, Johnny." "Hi." And "What are you playing with, Johnny?" He replied,

Success is not the result of spontaneous combustion. You must set yourself on fire.

—REGGIE LEACH

"Horse manure." "And what are you making with your horse manure?" "A principal," Johnny said.

"Uh-oh," the principal thought. "This child needs the school psychologist." The psychologist was a clever fellow who began by saying "Hi, Johnny." "Hi," said the boy. "I know what you are playing with, Johnny." "What?" asked Johnny. "Horse manure," said the psychologist. "Right," answered the boy. Then the psychologist said, "And I know what you're making with that horse manure." "What?" said the boy. "A psychologist!"

"Wrong," said the boy. "Not enough horse manure!"

When applying these principles of suffering to failure in business (or in sports, health, or any other field for that matter), we must redefine or "reframe" failure.

When Thomas Edison invented the light bulb, it is said that he accomplished it after one thousand attempts. When he was asked afterward how he felt while failing 999 times, he is said to have replied, "I didn't fail 999 times. I just found 999 ways of *not* inventing the light bulb!" Now that was reframing.

Another example is the fellow who comes into a supermarket and asks the clerk, "Where can I get a half grapefruit?" The clerk goes to the manager and says, "Some stupid jerk wants to know where he can get a half grapefruit." Just as he says this, he notices the man listening over his shoulder to every word he is saying to the manager. When the clerk realizes this, he says to the manager, "And this fine gentleman wants the other half!" Now, that's reframing!

When I told this story during a de Mello conference in

Love of others and love of ourselves are not alternatives. On the contrary, an attitude of love toward themselves will be found in all those who are capable of loving others.

—ERICH FROMM

Louisiana, a man came up to me and said, "Did you ever hear the end of that story?" I said no, I hadn't.

He said, "The manager told the young clerk, 'You know, you are pretty quick on your feet. I'm going to make you the manager of our store in Detroit.' 'Detroit,' says the clerk. 'The only things that come out of Detroit are prostitutes and hockey players.' 'Wait a minute,' says the manager, 'my wife comes from Detroit.' 'Oh,' says the clerk, 'what team did she play for?' " Again, that's reframing!

There is a lot to what Edison says and what these other examples illustrate. So much depends on how you look at things, how you perceive life, that determines your joy or misery, your success or failure. Not a bad insight. I have to remind myself of this constantly.

We will always have difficulties to overcome. Results are not always as we expect. Outcomes are not what we wanted or envisioned. My artist nephew says that often a finished painting differs greatly from what was first conceived—but can be infinitely more beautiful. Isn't that wonderful? Deepak Chopra says, "Desire the world, but don't become attached to the outcome of your desire."

Just as with happiness, you can never be grateful and unhappy at the same time. (These emotions simply cannot exist together.) So with suffering and failure. You cannot be grateful and fail at the same time. Start your day, every day, with this attitude of gratitude and watch the transformation your life will undergo.

Simply lift your head, look at the ceiling, and laugh. People may laugh if they hear you. What do you care? Just do it in the morning and before going to bed at night. Let those

Those things that hurt, instruct.

—BEN FRANKLIN

We are healed of a suffering only by experiencing it to the full.

—MARCEL PROUST

happy little molecules flow through your body. If you do this often enough, people will wonder why you always seem so content, pleasant, and genuinely happy. This practice of laughing gives you a new and wonderful perspective on life. I am told that in Japan they have "laughing clubs" where every morning, before work, the members meet in a park and have a twenty-minutes laughing session. It does wonders for their day.

Tony told the story of the abbot of a monastery who let out a roaring belly laugh every morning and every evening before retiring. The other monks never knew what he was laughing at, but were hesitant to ask him. So he died without ever telling them. Of course, you and I know why he was laughing.

How do you find happiness? By not going after it. If you make happiness your first order of business, you'll never find it. All you will get are thrills, excitement, and distractions, not abiding contentment. Happiness follows self-discovery. There is no possibility of it if you are a stranger to yourself. Position self-awareness before self-gratification.

On one occasion a man who had several hundred people working for him complained that he couldn't sit still long enough to meditate because he had so many things to do. Deepak Chopra amazed me by saying "Isn't that a revelation? You can be with others for hours and hours, but you are not comfortable to be with yourself for fifteen minutes!" Can you imagine a world without fear, where no one has the power to hurt you, where as a businessperson you have no fear of failing or losing to the competition? Imagine a spouse who is unafraid of husband or wife, children or relatives, or a workman

You can as well search for water without wetness, as an attachment without unhappiness.

—Anthony de Mello, S.J., *The Way to Love*

with no anxiety toward employer or friends. Imagine a single person with no loneliness or a citizen with no fear of a domineering government. Do you think such a world exists? It can exist for you. How? Life is a banquet, but most people are starving to death. Once off the coast of Brazil, people in a lifeboat were dying of thirst. Little did they know that they were in the Gulf Stream. The water beneath them was not ocean salt water but potable fresh drinking water. Here we are floating on oceans of happiness and we don't drink of it because we don't even realize it is there. We resemble the man who falls off a ladder and says, "It wasn't the fall that hurt me. It was the sudden stop!" It isn't life that hurts you; it's when life crashes against your fixed ideas and inflexible desires.

Here are two parables:

"What? Divorce my husband? I've spent thirty-five years with that rogue, and now you want me to make him happy?"

"I cannot tell you the number of my cabin on the ship, but I'd know it at once because it had a lighthouse outside the porthole!"

Like the ship, life moves on, my friend.

When you understand suffering and negative feelings, when you become an expert in handling them and see the growth they bring, you will find yourself looking forward to your next negative feeling and to the company of people who produce them.

You'll be like someone who has learned to fly. How he

The best and most beautiful things in the world can't be seen or even touched. They must be felt with the heart.

—HELEN KELLER

looks forward to that exhilarating experience. So will you look forward to everything that happens in life.

THREE THOUGHTS TO PONDER

1. Suffering is your imaginary picture of how things should be (or how you want them to be) clashing with what *actually* happens. As we just saw, suffering is desire clashing with reality. You are not appreciated, or you hope for a promotion, or you want to keep a friend. What happens? You are passed over. Someone else gets promoted. Your friend goes away. Your desires smash against the wall of reality. "The world is full of sorrow," says the Buddha. "The root of sorrow is desire. The uprooting of sorrow is desirelessness." Desires in themselves are good. They are energy. It's only when you make your happiness depend on them do they become "attachments." How do you deal with attachments? Realize that they spring from illusions. Say "I really do not need you for my happiness. I am only convincing myself I can't be happy without you."

2. The grand illusion: "I will be happy only if I can change these exterior affairs of my life. If I can change my job, my spouse, my state of life. If I have more money rather than less. If I have more respect from my coworkers, friends."

All of these equal the grand illusion. You change; *then* the world will change. Don't say "The world is right; therefore, I feel great." Say "I feel great; therefore, the world is fine!"

3. What people call happiness is nothing more than a pendulum. When something "favorable" happens in their exterior life—

We make a living by what we get. We make a life by what we give.

—WINSTON CHURCHILL

they receive money, compliments—"good feelings" result. When something negative happens—they experience fear, disappointment, rejection, loss, and death—a swing to depression results.

We swing back and forth, one end to the other, every day, every week of our lives.

You can enjoy life only when you finally attain what you know cannot be taken away or stolen. Consider the tourist who must keep his hand in his pocket to protect his wallet while he is exploring the sights. American Express developed this spiritual idea into a multibillion-dollar business: "Don't Leave Home Without It." Contrast the tourist with the farmer who has water in his well. The farmer is perfectly relaxed and isn't concerned or worried whether it rains or not.

There is no need to worry about where your good comes from, or *whether* it comes or not. You already have it.

LOVE

All emotions—fear, anger, joy, grief—have profound effects on our lives, both spiritually and physically, even medically. Nevertheless, the deepest emotion, so prominently discussed in Tony de Mello's conferences, is love. In one real sense love should not be classified as an emotion. It is truly a decision, not a feeling. But because love is so commonly thought of as the deepest of all emotions, I will leave it in that category. Despite the fact that writers pour out novels, poetry, and short stories about love, songwriters dedicate tunes to it, even spiritual masters say volumes about it, love is still tantalizingly elusive.

Why is this so? Because there are so many wrong-headed ideas about it, so much confusion. There are two major reasons for all this confusion. The first will take some time to spell out.

We tend to identify love with emotions or feelings that are associated with it but that are not its essence. For example, attraction is very much associated with love. I am drawn to you. I find you extremely attractive. But if love is only attraction, it comes and then soon dissipates. Do you recall the story of Grandma and Grandpa, sitting on the porch after having celebrated their sixtieth wedding anniversary. Grandpa says to Grandma, "I admire you," and Grandma says, "What did you say?" "I said [louder] Grandma, I admire you." And Grandma says, "You have to speak a lot louder, my hearing is going. What did you say?" "I said [shouting] Grandma, I admire you." She said, "That's okay, I'm tired of you too." There's also a wonderful Irish story about Pat and Mike. Pat says to Mike, "Mike, we're going into this jungle to do some hunting, but suppose a snake bites me?" Mike says to Pat, "Well, that problem is solved simply. What you do is you take your knife out of your scabbard, you cut across your snake bite, and you suck out the poisonous blood right from the wound." "Oh!" says Pat. "What happens if the snake bites me on the arse?" "Ah, then," says Mike, "that's when you find out who your true friends really are."

Other emotions also can be associated with love. People feel so strongly, deeply, about someone or something that they say that they love the person or thing. It's very easy to confuse love with strong emotion because the feelings are so profound. Some time ago they showed on TV a film called *Substitute Wife*. The story begins with the wife of a farmer in the

Midwest in the nineteenth century discovering that she has a terminal illness and will soon die. Her husband doesn't even want to think about it, much less talk about it. However, she insists that because they have small children, they do need to prepare. She says she must find someone he should wed after she dies, to care for the children and for him. She finally brings home a widow to introduce to the husband. Because women are scarce in the town, it is not easy to find someone suitable.

After the farmer, having dressed up himself and the children, meets the widow, he declares he will not marry her. Later on, in private, the wife angrily asks why. He replies, "She doesn't raise a tingle in me." This infuriates the wife, but suddenly she stops her tirade and in one of the most poignant scenes asks, "Do I raise a tingle in you?" Turning toward her, he looks directly in her eyes and replies, "Every time I lay my eyes on you!"

The scene still brings tears to the eyes of strong men.

A humorous story illustrates the considerable confusion that surrounds feelings of love. A boy has a little pet turtle who lives in a lake. One day the boy visits the lake and finds the turtle on his back with his legs up. Assuming this is the end of his turtle, he starts to cry and runs back home to tell his mother and dad that Mr. Turtle has died and he's very upset. The father says to him, "You know, these things do happen, son, but I'll tell you what we'll do. We'll go down and build a little grave for him. We'll get Mr. Undertaker to build a little picket fence and bury him in the grave."

So the boy gets excited about this ritual. Down they go, the mother, the father, the maid, and the boy marching to the lake. But they can't find the turtle. Suddenly they look out

When his shoe dropped as the train started,
Gandhi took off the other and dropped that one
also. "So that the poor man who finds the first
one will have a pair."

onto the lake, and there's the turtle swimming around, having a merry time. When the boy sees this, he turns to his father and says, "Let's kill him!"

Now, who was the boy in love with? Was he in love with love itself, or was he in love with the turtle? In both cases, strong feelings are closely associated with love.

Often you hear it said from people who deeply love each other, "I can't live without you; we depend completely on each other." These statements about love sound very complimentary, but when you examine them, you notice the flaws. "I need you." If my life, my happiness, really depends on you, then I am going to manipulate you in such a way that I'll never, never let you go. I'll never lose you.

By contrast, true love includes being happy without the other. Thus you can enjoy your relationship to the fullest. This situation resembles enjoying a place where you have lived and worked. If you really enjoyed it, when you return to it there is no nostalgia; you have drained it of all emotion.

Another old saw says, "Love is blind." On the contrary, there is nothing so clear-sighted as love. You've never truly loved anyone, the spiritual masters say, only your image of them. That's why genuine love is clarity of perception, accuracy of response.

Love is never coercive. It never demands a return of love. No, love is its own reward. It is not a thing of the marketplace. For example, if I give you a gift for your birthday and then say, "By the way, next week is my birthday," that's not love, that's a bribe.

The story is told about Juliana of Norwich, a famous mystic of the Middle Ages, who had a vision of Jesus on the cross.

Once you can accept your own death, all of a sudden you're free to live. You no longer care about your reputation. You no longer care except so far as your life can be used tactically—to promote a cause you believe in.

—SAUL ALINSKY

Jesus asked her, "Do you know why I hang on the cross, Juliana?"

And she said, "Yes, Lord."

"And do you know that I hang on the cross for the love of you?"

"Yes, Lord."

"And does it please you that I love you so much?"

"Yes, Lord."

And when He had heard her reply, she said, "Jesus raised His head and laughed right merrily on the cross."

Now he didn't say, "Oh, Juliana, aren't you going to hang on the cross for me as well?" No. Jesus raised His head and laughed right merrily on the cross.

The other reason we're confused about love is this: *We fail to realize that love is a mystery.* As with God and truth, you cannot say what love is—only what it is not. There are analogies, but that's what they are, only comparisons. Allow me to paraphrase what St. Thomas Aquinas said about God: "This much is certain, whatever you say about God is more wrong than right." Such also can be said of love. Love is mystery. Even the important Church document by the Fourth Lateran Council (A.D. 1215) alludes to this: ". . . between creator and creature there can be noted no similarity so great that a greater dissimilarity cannot be seen between them."

BECOMING LOVING

The question may arise, "How do you become loving?"

The answer is "Don't try, become real. Don't be disillu-

The teacher gives not of his wisdom but rather of his faith and lovingness.

—Khalil Gibran

sioned by the myths about loving." For example, consider the monkey that saved the fish from drowning by putting him on a branch. As the fish squirmed to return to the water, the monkey said, "All I was trying to do was save you from drowning."

God save us from the do-gooders in life!

BECOMING REAL

So how do you become real? By looking, seeing, becoming sensitive to all creation. Do this and you'll become real yourself. You won't have to work at being loving. Love will grasp you in its warm embrace.

Can a rose withhold its fragrance from the bad and give it only to the good? Can a lamp shine only on the kind and compassionate and withhold its light from evildoers? Can a tree withhold its shade from the evil ones and give it only to the doers of good? No. And as the poet Kabir says, "Even if it is cut down, if it is a sweet-smelling tree, it will leave its scent on the ax."

Stories abound to illustrate the mystery of love. For example, consider the soldier who asks to go search for one of his wounded buddies. And the commander says to him, "No, permission denied. If you go out, you might be killed, and we don't even know if the man is alive." However, the soldier goes out anyway and when he comes back, he has the body of his buddy in his arms, but he himself has been mortally wounded.

Exasperated, the commander says to him, "Now do you see how stupid that was? Now I've lost both of you." But the soldier says, "No. When I got there, Joe was still alive and he said to me, 'Bill, I knew you'd come.' "

How can you explain that kind of illogical thinking except in terms of the mystery of love?

In a fine book, *D-Day, 1944,* author Theodore A. Wilson says that the soldiers were told not to care for the wounded during the invasion of Normandy because they themselves might be killed. Yet they did. The success of the invasion, he says, was in fact attributed to the spirit of caring for one's buddy during a venture that never should have succeeded, given the powerful forces against it.

Then why did the D-Day invasion succeed? Patriotism, yes, but more the sense of not letting one's brother down, of being filled with a magnificent sense of love for one another.

Of course, the story that really touches my heart concerns Father Flanagan. Not too long ago, I visited Father Flanagan's crypt and was moved to read those words written on it, the famous words that he always used at Boys Town: "There is no such thing as a bad boy."

Here is a true story about a young and violent boy. Although he was only eight years old, he had killed his mother and his father. The Chicago police didn't want to put him in prison because they felt he was too young, but they also didn't want him out on the street because they felt he was too violent. So they decided to take him to Boys Town to see Father Flanagan.

Years later the boy wrote in his journal how well he remembered that trip on the train. He said to himself, "They're bringing me to some priest. If he tells me he loves me, I'll kill him." When he got there, he met Father Flanagan, who said,

"Well, hello, Joe, this is James and Bill. They'll show you around. Everyone does his own part here, all pitch in." The boy said that moment with Father Flanagan changed his life, transformed him forever, because "I saw in his eyes not 'I love you,' but 'You are good.' " Because of this, his whole life was forever transformed.

"Don't Change"

I cited earlier the powerful story "Don't Change" from Tony de Mello's book *Song of the Bird*. In the story, a person was depressed by the fact that he was unable to change. He was cured only when someone told him he was loved whether he changed or not.

When I tell that story I always like to end by asking the question, "Do you think God loves you that way?" Of course He does, everyone agrees with that, but that's not the point of the story. The point is that you have to find someone who will love you whether you change or not, and that someone has to be *yourself*. You must look into a mirror and say, "I love you, don't change. I love you just as you are." And when you reach that stage, then you know that change will take place.

An Englishman and a Scotsman were lost in the snowy Alps. They saw a St. Bernard dog heading toward them with a cask of cognac around his neck. "Look!" said the Englishman. "Man's best friend."

"Yes," said the Scotsman, "and look at that wonderful dog that's bringing it."

So much depends on your own perspective.

It is vital to teach Johnny and Mary how to read and write and think and compute. But if they don't learn to love themselves and each other, the rest isn't worth anything. Self-esteem and the capacity for loving are the most basic skills each human being has the need and right to learn about.

—DR. CARL ROGERS

SPIRITUALITY IN RELATIONSHIPS WITH FRIENDS AND BUSINESS ASSOCIATES

The spiritual principles that govern your relationships with coworkers are the same that operate in your personal life with spouse, friend, or neighbor. The spiritual dimension and the power of love are at the root of all these relationships and must be examined closely. Love should not be taken for granted. One might ask: How can a spiritual director offer advice on improving relationships with coworkers? My own response is modest, grounded in the fact that you don't have to be able to lay an egg in order to tell a good one from a rotten one. All I know is that every day I work at improving my relationships with everyone around me, and in the course of that I have discovered certain spiritual principles that work for me. I share these principles with you so you can apply them to your own situation.

In the Scriptures, John the Evangelist says, "How can you say you love God if you don't love your neighbor?" But I ask: How can you say you love your neighbor unless you have learned to love yourself? Why we find it so difficult to love ourselves can be the subject of a whole book.

First of all, we are well educated in *not* loving ourselves. Our education and upbringing, what our parents, teachers, coaches, tell us, amounts to: "You are simply not good enough." We are taught to identify with our careers or names, our reputations, bodies, and youth. Of course, when anything

Folk who never do more than they get paid to do, never get paid for any more than they do.

—ELBERT HUBBARD

goes awry in these areas, we say, "I am depressed," "I am a loser," "I am fat, balding, and unattractive."

The truth of the matter is: You are extraordinary, unique. You are a treasure; you have power beyond your wildest imaginings. But we find it hard to believe this. We have been so carefully taught; it's in our bloodstream, our neural connections, like those kittens in the experiment that had no neural connections in their brains to enable them to sense anything vertical.

That's why people find meditating, praying in silence, so difficult. They cannot be quiet for any length of time. Not because they are unable to be quiet, but because they are so uncomfortable being alone with themselves. If they don't know who they are, how *can* they be comfortable? And then, still not knowing who they are, they're asked to love themselves. I want to stress some basics about love that you can apply to loving yourself and *then* to strengthening your relationships with others.

The reason so much confusion about love exists is that we tend to identify love with attraction and the feeling of being in love, able to depend on someone with mutuality, meaning, of course, that such love demands a return, as if it were an investment. The attraction passes, yet love remains. I may be drawn or attracted to you, but that doesn't last. If I have identified love with that attraction, when the attraction ceases, there goes love and the relationship. True love is not blind, because nothing is so clear-sighted as love. Clarity of perception, accuracy of response—there is no better definition of love.

Let me frame these thoughts in a few practical principles.

The meaning of communication is the response you get.

—NEUROLINGUISTIC PROGRAMMING PRINCIPLE

1. Don't enter a relationship, either personal or business, in order to get something out of it.

Ask yourself: What can I give to this relationship, friendship, business association? As John F. Kennedy said in his inaugural speech, "Fellow countrymen, ask not what your country can do for you, ask what you can do for your country." If I enter into a relationship to solve my problems, I have already sown the seeds for destruction of that relationship. If I enter a relationship to change myself or those around me, I am disempowering myself and those around me. If, however, I notice how I can contribute to that relationship, I am always coming from a strong base, and those around me will be prompted to do the same in return.

2. Recognize and work against two negative forces that harm relationships personally or at work.

These two forces are taking others for granted and allowing negative anchors.

As for the first: If you are around anything or anyone long enough, a certain boredom sets in. The sparkle of initial experience that made the person feel so very alive, excited, energetic seems to fade. If you get caught up in the details of work, you may forget to foster the relationship. Just being aware of this happening can go far toward reducing it. Recall the story of Grandma and Grandpa I've already told.

As for the second: Develop an acute sensitivity to the power of what, in psychology, is called "anchoring." Whenever you experience an intense emotional experience, your brain tends to link such emotions to the persons around you

We become what we think about.

—EARL NIGHTINGALE

associated with them. Examples are a death in the family, a job promotion, or failure of a business venture. If you anchor or link these feelings to *people*, whenever you see the people, you recall these feelings: sadness or disappointment for negative feelings and joy or excitement for positive ones.

Be aware that negative anchors, more than anything else, tend to destroy relationships. For example, if you argue with a spouse or close friend and get into a tense state, you will begin to link this upset to whoever is around you.

What should you do? Have a spirited argument, but keep it short. Don't let the argument end with a lasting anger. If you do, you will anchor your anger to that person and whenever you see him or her, just the sight will arouse your anger. Remember the slogan: Don't let the sun set on your anger. It's good advice.

Find ways to stop an argument. Agree beforehand on your strategy. Tony Robbins in his book *Ultimate Power* calls it "interrupting your pattern." You agree beforehand that when a certain phrase is said, you stop the argument and do something else. Thus you take definite action to improve the situation. Some people think they can walk away from the situation in a huff: "I've had it!" "You'll never understand!" The main problem with this move is that you take the argument along with you.

3. Learn strategies to create happiness and joy in your various relationships.

What triggers others to be happy when they are around you? Some people need to hear praise from you. Some need to see it by an action—for example, being taken out for lunch.

To fall into a habit is to begin to cease to be.

—MIGUEL DE UNAMUNO

Some may even need a physical touch, a pat on the back. But remember, some people in relationships (including you!) may react more to how they visualize the other person; others to how the other person sounds to them; others to the bodily movements or gestures they pick up from the other person. Dr. Phil McGraw, who frequently appears on Oprah Winfrey's show, offers excellent ideas on this point in his book *Relationship Rescue*. He is worth watching and reading.

WAKING UP: THREE STORIES

The question on my mind, which I know lives in the minds of most people, is: Once you realize that spirituality means waking up from our insane world, a world programmed into our minds by our parenting, by our education, even by our religion, how can you achieve it? By what means?

Let me go back for a minute to the three stories Tony told in Chapter One. I consider them the heart and soul of this book.

The first story described the magic moment that Helen Keller was able to make a connection between the water she felt flowing from the pump onto her hand and the "signing" Annie Sullivan was trying to teach her: w-a-t-e-r. It was a moment in which everything came together. What I'm saying is that, when you do the various exercises suggested in this book, know that the time will come when a similar breakthrough will happen to you. What you thought and prayed about, what you meditated on, *will* make sense to you.

Common sense is not so common.

—Voltaire

The second two stories are about the freedom you need for any authentic spirituality. There's the story of the ascetic who fasted from morning to sundown daily, consuming no food or water; he took the presence of a bright star above a nearby mountain as a sign of divine approval. One day he climbs the mountain along with a small village girl. She gets terribly thirsty but won't drink water unless he does. He is torn, but finally breaks his fast for the girl's sake. He's covered with guilt, but lo, that night *two* stars appear above the mountain. And then there's the story of the guru who tells a disciple the mantra that liberates anyone who knows it from the bondage of ignorance and suffering; but at the same time he warns the disciple never to tell it to anyone else; if he does, he will be damned. The disciple is so delighted at his own release from bondage that he blabs the mantra to the whole town. Instead of damning him, his guru promotes him to the rank of guru.

The lesson is clear. Both the ascetic and the disciple are free from rigidity and inflexibility, as well as from external pressures. This allows them to make the same kind of breakthrough we saw with Helen Keller.

And the rest of us? Most of us are living a life of addiction to our past—its mistakes and the guilt we carry—or to a future that drives us like a tyrant. The beautiful moment that is the present passes us by. We never realize or get in touch with the fine time we have right now.

Late I have loved, oh beauty ever ancient, ever new. Late have I loved you. You were within, but I was outside. You were within, but I was not with you.

—ST. AUGUSTINE

DISPOSITIONS NEEDED FOR AWAKENING

The first disposition is to admit that you're asleep, not in touch with reality. It's difficult because we have been programmed to believe that this dream state we live in, this hypnotic state, is real. In any addiction of whatever form, one of the prime elements is denial. If you ever attend a Twelve-Step Program, the first step to recovery is admitting that you are powerless over alcohol, the drug, or the eating, depending on the program involved.

The second disposition is to be able to listen. Sometimes we consider listening to be easy, but do we listen in order to discover something, or merely to confirm what we already believe?

You may know the story about a man who goes into a bar and sees a person with a banana in his ear? Although he thinks to himself, "Maybe I should tell him," he doesn't. He sits down and finally, after a martini or two, he decides, "I will tell that guy!" So he walks over to the man and says, "By the way, do you know you have a banana in your ear?" The man says, "Can you speak a little louder please?" So the first man says, "I said, do you realize you have a banana in your ear?" The man replies, "You're gonna have to speak a lot louder. You know I have a banana in my ear." Listening, then, along with getting past all the denial, will prepare us better for the moment of awakening we all desire.

five

Contemporary Catholic:

Live TV Interview about Prayer

In his lifetime of spiritual conferences and talks, Tony de Mello did not like to be recorded or videotaped. Although this was his general rule, he did make exceptions. One exception he enthusiastically embraced was a live television interview with Sister Dorothy Farley in 1985 on WOR-TV (Channel 9 in New York City). The program was called *Contemporary Catholic*. The interview was enormously successful and received a great deal of positive audience response, even when it was rerun months later.

In this interview, Tony's ideas on prayer were admirably expressed. What follows is an exact transcript of that program, provided by Sister Dorothy herself. Had it not been for his untimely death, there would have been many more programs and interviews. I have a letter in my files from Bill Moyers, one of the most respected journalists in contemporary television, saying, "I have put Tony on my 'must be done' list"!

SISTER F: Prayer is the easiest thing in the world to do, although at times the most difficult. It was defined long ago as the lifting up of our minds and hearts to God. If prayer is that simple, then why don't we pray more? Why don't we pray better?

Our guest today is a priest from the Sadhana Institute in Pune, India. Father Anthony de Mello is a Jesuit priest, director of the Sadhana Institute. He is known in many countries for retreats, workshops, and seminars on prayer.

You made a statement at one of your workshops that everybody is tired of "God-talk." What did you mean by that?

TDM: Let me put it this way. If you went to a restaurant and they gave you the menu, and kept giving you beautiful menus, nicely painted, and you started eating the menu, you would get pretty tired of that. Suppose you look at the menu and see "beefsteak." Now, you want the beefsteak, you don't want the words. We tend to talk about God, but I think what everybody's hungry for is not God-talk, they're hungry for God. They're tired of the menu, they want something substantial to eat.

SR. F: That raises a lot of questions. How do we find God without the menu? And don't we have a lot of trouble doing that? Who is God?

TDM: Now, that's interesting. Maybe one of the biggest obstacles to our finding God is that we think we know so much about Him. You remember how people were looking

The consciousness of divinity comes only with quietude.

— MEISTER ECKHART

for the Messiah and when the Messiah came, they missed Him because they had a fixed concept of who the Messiah was. When they saw this person there they said, "You mean this is the Messiah?"

In the East we have a nice story. A little fish moves around in the ocean, searching for it. Whenever he meets another fish he says, "Where can I find the ocean? " The other fish says, "The ocean? *This* is the ocean!" But the little fish says, "This is water, I'm looking for the ocean."

Now that's what's happening with so many people who are looking for God. It's like they're surrounded by Him everywhere, but they don't recognize him because they're looking for the wrong thing, they're looking in the wrong place.

SR. F: Two things I want to ask you. I don't know whether to be negative first and say what not to look for, or what to look for.

TDM: All right. Let's begin with what to look for.

SR. F: All right.

TDM: The first thing would be, don't look for anything. Because if you're looking for something, the danger is you will miss what you're really looking for. It's like you're looking so hard for something and you've got an idea of what that thing is in your mind. Now, one of the great qualities of God is that He's so unpredictable. He keeps coming up in forms in which you don't expect to see Him, and you're taken by surprise. So, first of all, don't look too hard. And don't look for any fixed idea you have in your mind. My advice to people is, if you would get into silence and just become present, you can't miss it. It's all there.

MASTER: *As the fish dies on the land, so you die in the midst of worldly business. To live again, the fish returns to water. You must return to solitude.*

DISCIPLE: *Must I therefore leave my business and go to a monastery?*

MASTER: *Certainly not. Hold on to your business and go back to your heart.*

—TONY DE MELLO

SR. F: It sounds rather difficult since we're talking in New York, a city that's constantly moving. I think we all are too. To be silent and to find time for silence amid noise is a real challenge.

TDM: All right. That's a real objection. But you know, Dorothy, the silence I'm talking about is not the kind of silence of the monastery. To my mind, you can have it in the marketplace. You know, like you and I are talking now and both of us could be very silent, even while we're talking. *By being silent, I mean be right here, right now.* Be aware of what's happening to you right now, like I'm talking to you right now, and I'm aware of what I'm doing. That's silence.

SR. F: That takes some practice.

TDM: Well, you can try it right now.

SR. F: All right.

TDM: I can understand you in the United States, especially when you're talking about New York. I walk along the streets of New York and it's impressive: the efficiency, the drive of the people. I wouldn't say you should stop that in order to obtain God. Just keep doing what you're doing. Let's suppose you're driving a car. You can be silent while driving a car. You're sitting right here, right now. Now just be aware of your back pressing against the chair. We're on TV right now. Lots of people out there are listening to us, and they can do the same thing. Be aware of the feel of the chair pressing against your back. Or your thighs pressing on the chair. Be aware of your hands resting on the chair arms. Are you aware of that right now? What do you feel if you become aware of it? Take just a few seconds to become aware. What happens to you?

What is the most important question a human being has to answer: Is the universe a friendly place or not?

—ALBERT EINSTEIN

SR. F: Well, I think first there's a struggle to get rid of everything else.

TDM: Ah, that's it. All right.

SR. F: 'Cause I want to think of the next thing.

TDM: That's it!

SR. F: "What am I going to ask Tony next?" is on my mind.

TDM: I can see that, yes. Now, what you're saying is what happens to *most* people. We're not here, we're thinking what's going to come next. You're very honest. You're saying, What am I going to ask him next, which means you're not here, which means you're going to find it hard to let go, relax, be in the present. Now, as soon as you deal with that struggle, you become silent, relaxed. That, I think, is the great beauty of silence and of prayer. If you would let go, become relaxed and present, there's a whole wellspring of energy that would keep coming out of you. You would be amazed at how much work you could get done with a minimum of energy.

I think what's really happening to people is that they're driving with the brakes on. See, you have a nice expression here in the States. You're driving, but you've got your brakes on. Now think of the amount of energy that takes. Whereas when you take your foot off the brakes, off that pedal, you flow. So you get much more work done with a minimum expenditure of energy.

SR. F: All right. Now I have the next question.

TDM: Good.

SR. F: And that is, am I going to do the kind of thing you exhorted me to do? To feel the chair, feel the back, to go

You never get a second chance to make a first impression.

through this for a much extended period of time than we did here, right?

TDM: Yes . . . ?

SR. F: Am I going to do that at certain times during the day? Every once in a while doing that? How does it work together with the flow of the whole day?

TDM: Let me think of a concrete situation. Suppose you're driving your car. Now, you get the feel of your body resting on the car seat, the feel of the steering wheel. You're very conscious of the road and what's happening. You can be very conscious of what I'm saying right now and yet you can get the feel of this chair seat. So, every time you remember it, get in touch with your body, with any sensations you feel. That's a good way of getting into the present.

Or, let's say you've had dinner and you're doing the dishes. Now, if you could feel that water, you could be quite effective with the dishes. Feel that water flowing through your fingers, get the feel of the dish as you're washing. There, once again, you're quieting down, coming to the present, because you know you'll find it impossible to be doing this and to be worrying about the future or anxious about the past. At least, for a brief moment, you're right into the present. Now, what's likely to happen is that you'll forget about it, as happens to most people. But then every time you remember it, you come back to it, and after a while, you develop an appetite for this. So these brief moments of silence keep multiplying. The next thing you know, a month or two has [sic] passed. You've done the same amount of work, but you're more relaxed. You've got more energy; you've "come home" and you're not so tense. So prayer, in this sense of silence, is one of the most effective, useful, and practical things in modern life.

SR. F: Is that exercise the prayer itself? Or does the prayer flow from it?

TDM: If you can get into the present, really be there and taste silence, that *is* the prayer of the great contemplative. You know, the taste of silence. Because you become silent, it's impossible to get into silence without tasting something of what we call God, the Divine, the ground of our being. Now, that would be prayer, a very good prayer. You needn't think Now I've got to talk to God.

SR. F: We're always looking for words.

TDM: That's right, and that would be fine. It's excellent because you know the human heart needs to communicate. So there will be times when you will talk to God. But suppose you really love someone, then you're just there, silent. There's no need to talk. Now, that's the kind of silence I mean. You'd be still, sometimes not even conscious anyone is there. But if you become silent, something has happened. While it's happening, you won't be conscious of it—until later—but it's all there.

SR. F: There's something else you said that struck me. About us in relationship to prayer so, in a sense, we're all businessmen rather than mystics.

TDM: All right. How will I explain that? You know, there are two types of people: There's the businessman and there's the person who's all alive celebrating. But one needs both types. What do I mean by a businessman? I mean someone who has a goal he's got to work toward. He's got a purpose, an aim. Now, that's wonderful because, thanks to that, you've got skyscrapers here and jumbo jets, all these modern inventions that I see here in the States. Every time I come here it's a kind of culture shock, but it's wonderful, beautiful.

But now, there's something else that we need to develop at the same time. We need the capacity of celebrating, of living. Not just living in order to do something, but living, just being here. Let me give you an example. I told you about washing those dishes, remember?

SR. F: I don't know that I'll be convinced it's a good thing to do.

TDM: You mean, washing the dishes?

SR. F: Yes! *[laughs]*

TDM: *[laughs]* So now you've got those dishes. Suppose you wash those dishes because you're going to have dinner. You've invited guests, and your mind and everything are geared to that dinner. So it's like, Let's hurry up and do these dishes, but the dishes have no importance, the washing has no importance, your mind is all on that dinner. Now, that's business. You're washing the dishes in order to get something.

But now, suppose that although I've got that dinner coming, I still want to enjoy the feel of washing these dishes. So, when you're washing, you're *really* washing the dishes, you're all there. Now you're something of a mystic, a celebrant. You're tasting life, living life. If your only aim in peeling an orange is to eat the orange, what's likely to happen is that when eating the orange, you won't be eating the orange. You'll be somewhere else, thinking of something else.

SR. F: Always!

TDM: You're always somewhere else.

SR. F: Or back.

What is to give light must endure burning.

—VIKTOR FRANKL

————————————

Pain is the bitter pill of the inner physician that cracks the shell of our understanding. And, after all, how can a seed grow into a flower unless the seed swells and dies?

—KHALIL GIBRAN

TDM: Or back. So the strange thing is that you've had a glorious dinner, but you haven't eaten it because you were not there but somewhere else.

SR. F: I have another question. The dishes are not terribly bad. I'm not convinced I like doing them. But what about things we *really* don't like, very unpleasant circumstances, or pain? I want to forget about that, so do I really want to be present for that, aware of that pain?

TDM: Now, that's a tough question. You're good at questions, I must say.

SR. F: *[laughs]* I was thinking ahead.

TDM: *[laughs]* So, now I give two answers. Let me tell you something that I experienced. I was once making a retreat under a Buddhist guru. I was keen on finding out what Buddhist meditation is all about. This man said to us, "I want you to take a posture and keep it for an hour; don't move."

Well, I was sitting in a kind of semilotus posture that's quite difficult and I thought I'll manage about ten minutes but not more. But I was determined not to move although I had tremendous pain in my right knee and in my back. I was thinking, "Shall I change my posture and get rid of the pain or shall I be right here?" Now, he had also said to us that when you feel a pain, don't run away from it, get into it, so to speak. So I thought, "Maybe I'll give it a try." So I got into my knee, this pain there, and I tried to break it up into its various component parts. A warmth, a pulling sensation, a pushing sensation, various sensations, and a point there that I identified as the pain, which kept moving from one place to another. And you know what happened to me?

At the end of that one hour, I was still in pain but *no suf-*

Great men are they who see that the spiritual is stronger than any material force, that thoughts rule the world.

—RALPH WALDO EMERSON

fering. Because what is suffering? Suffering is "I don't want this! I want to get rid of it! I want to run away from it! How long is this going to last?" But as soon as you can accept something (by "accept," I don't say approve of it, enjoy it, or even be resigned to it), you can just be with it, not run away from it. If you can rid yourself of it, fine, but as long as it's there, you're peaceful with it. That's when you get the experience of pain without suffering. Now, if you can do this, it brings great spiritual depth in you as a person.

But I promised you two answers to that question. I wouldn't recommend this to everybody, all the time. If the pain gets too intense, then do something to kill it. But take the pain in small doses and as you get accustomed to it, you'll be amazed. If somebody had said this to me before I did that retreat, I would have thought he was crazy. Just as if somebody had said to me, some fifteen years ago, all that you need to get into silence and into prayer is just to be present to your body. I would have thought, "Oh, that's too silly. That's too superficial."

SR. F: We're not used to that.

TDM: Right. It's so simple that we don't believe it. We think it should be difficult.

SR. F: What about other prayers, though? We have a whole history, the liturgy itself, the rosary, other kinds of prayers. Do we still use those?

TDM: Yes. The liturgy is very beautiful, plus all these other prayers we say. They fill a need of the human heart. We need to communicate to God in this way, with our minds, our bodies, our emotions, and as a group in a community. But most of the day, you can't be doing that. Like when you're driving a

Why do angels fly? Because they take themselves lightly.

—TONY ROBBINS

car. Like when I'm talking to you right now, quite aware of what I'm doing and saying, aware of the feel of my body. I can hardly be talking to God, and yet I can be silent, get into silence while I'm talking to you. So I can do both things.

There are times when we need to speak. Like when you're in distress, you spontaneously cry out to God. That's beautiful. And then times when there is no need to say anything. You're just there. The beauty of it is, you don't have to stop your action, your activity. This Buddhist retreat master of ours was very interesting. He would give retreats to dozens of priests, sisters, ministers, and people of other religions too. Imagine my surprise when I found he was an industrialist, a very wealthy industrialist. He said to me that ever since he got into this kind of silence, the silent way of meditation, his business began to improve. I can see why. Because outside, he was working very actively, but inside, he was resting, relaxed. Whatever he was doing, *he* wasn't doing it. It was being done through him and he was letting go. What I'm suggesting is for every day, see?

But one also needs to take time out for the liturgy.

SR. F: Before we get too far, however, I want to mention your book *Sadhana* because it contains so many useful exercises.

TDM: That's right.

SR. F: I plan on trying many of them. I'd like to ask too, if somebody reads the book and follows the exercises, can he or she guide others into doing them individually, or with a group?

TDM: Do them with a group. However, if you want to guide somebody, you need to have experienced what you're

The only thing that we can know is that we know nothing. And that is the highest flight of wisdom.

—LEO TOLSTOY

talking about. Unless you've experienced all of this, it would be better not to venture into guiding other people. But to do with others what I suggest in the book, first read it aloud to them. Then get them to do it. That's fine.

Or you can do it yourself, you know. The book is self-explanatory. Just read the text and do an exercise; read the text and do an exercise.

SR. F: Do you advocate not doing it alone, or am I being too negative in saying that?

TDM: No, no. In fact, this book was written for individual use. You read a chapter and then do an exercise. However, it's use by a group or a couple is valuable. If you can get somebody to read an exercise to you slowly, you know, it's a kind of community silence, even deeper.

SR. F: What about the place?

TDM: To my mind, anyplace, provided the noise around is not so shattering to damage your ear. Anyplace is really good for this kind of prayer. Oh, maybe for those fantasy exercises you need a more silent place. But for the first part of the book, the awareness exercises, the noise doesn't disturb. Just be aware of the noise and how the noise creates silence.

SR. F: I really wish that we had more time, especially because you have some wonderful things in your previous book, *The Song of the Bird*.

TDM: Oh, yes, the stories.

SR. F: But if we had more time, it would mean you couldn't return to India. We'd have to keep you here in New York.

TDM: *[laughs]* Yes, I must get back tomorrow.

SR. F: I want to thank you very much for being with us.

When the gods want to punish us, they answer our prayers.

—OSCAR WILDE

six

The Rescue Triangle

A process that Tony used in his workshops is called "the Rescue Triangle." It's a practical problem in which many of us get involved in subtle ways. He took the triangle from Eric Berne's book, *Games People Play*. "A game," says Berne, "is an ongoing series of complementary, ulterior transactions progressing to a well-defined, predictable outcome. Every game is basically dishonest."

Tony would say that a game is a transaction between two people when one is attempting to give the other unconsciously a not-okay feeling and to get the other to give him or both of them a not-okay feeling. And the evidence is a strange quirkiness, this not-okay feeling that people first gave us in childhood. We were spanked for being bold children; we were told we were born in original sin. So we go through life

Half the world is composed of people who have something to say and can't, and the other half who have nothing to say and keep on saying it.

—ROBERT FROST

getting this confirmed. To seek further proof of this, we develop what Berne calls the "NIGYYSOAB" syndrome: "Now I've got you, you son of a bitch."

In the Rescue Triangle scenario, the participants play the roles of rescuer, victim, and persecutor. This can be diagrammed as a triangle, with the R, V, and P on each corner of the triangle. The genuine rescuer is one who goes out to help a victim who is completely incapable of helping himself or herself. For example, a person who is unconscious, or a newborn baby. Most people, though, can do a great deal to help themselves. Situations when you need someone from outside to help are extremely rare.

So, who is the game-playing rescuer? People play this role in one of four instances: (1) you go to help someone who doesn't want or need your help; (2) you help someone *you* do not want to help; (3) you help someone but he or she is not doing everything in his or her power to help him- or herself; and (4) you help someone who wants something but doesn't express his or her wants.

Generally, the favorite emotions connected with each person are: guilt in the rescuer; helplessness and resentment in the victim; resentment and anger in the persecutor.

So I become a rescuer when I give you help that you do not want or you do not need. For example, in 1936 Thomas Roberts was appointed the Archbishop of Bombay, although he had no understanding of India. When he found a highly developed church, a gifted clergy, and twenty-five bishops, he began asking, "What am I doing here? Me, an Englishman transplanted when there are plenty of people here that are suitable." In fact, a concordat existed: Bishops in India were either English

Don't sweat the small stuff. And it's all small stuff.

—Richard Carlson

or Portuguese. In other words, the Bombay bishop had to be English, and when he died, they would put in a Portuguese bishop. This caused a tremendous resentment in the local church because the Indian people were being given help they didn't need or they didn't want. This situation happens frequently in the missions because deep down people hate being helped. Though often grateful, people are resentful.

Of course, the true solution is to escape the whole thing, but sometimes you're just stuck, as Roberts was. But he was different. He resorted to a subterfuge. In 1946 he appointed an auxiliary bishop by the name of Gracias (pronounced "Gracious"). And then in 1947 Roberts sailed away, disappeared, after having told Gracias to run the diocese. After five years, it was clear that Roberts wasn't returning. So the Vatican decided to appoint a successor archbishop. By the way, this occurred three years after India's independence from Great Britain. Somehow the news leaked to Prime Minister Nehru, who decided that no foreign archbishop would be allowed to set foot on Indian soil. He simply wouldn't get a visa. Finally in 1950 the Vatican appointed Gracias as archbishop of the diocese. If you apply all this to spiritual direction, what you really want is to get the other person to think for him- or herself. But such thinking generally means challenging you. That's why sometimes really great spiritual people do not have spiritual directors or spiritual healers, although they occasionally seek help. So growing up is all about taking responsibility for oneself.

Now consider the second rescuer. In the first instance you help someone who doesn't need or want your help. The second instance occurs when you yourself don't want to give the

The greatest evil that can befall a man is that he should come to think evil of himself.

—JOHANN VON GOETHE

help. Suppose someone comes to you and says, "Could I have a word with you?" Suppose you're actually too tired? Ah, but shouldn't you always feel available to friends? "See me after supper." But when the person comes and talks only about small matters, then you move from feeling rescuer to feeling the victim. If you get irritable, then you become the persecutor. In the end, the client or the person sees you now in a bad light, not as a helper.

So you must have the guts to say no when you mean no.

The third rescuer is the person who helps someone who is not doing all they can to help themselves. Someone has asked you to do something, but here he is, reading a novel. He asked you to paint his house, but there he sits, reading on the lawn.

The fourth situation involving the Rescue Triangle occurs when someone wants something from you but doesn't make it clear what he or she wants. For example, tomorrow is Mother's birthday, but she doesn't say, "I want someone to make breakfast for me, clean the house."

Unconsciously what this person does, by not honestly expressing requests or feelings, is to set a trap. When nothing happens, the person has bitter feelings, becomes a victim, then a kind of persecutor. If such a person is asked, "Why didn't you say what you wanted, but also leave people free to do what they wanted?," they may reply, "But if you love me, you would have done this and that." Such a person is bent on being loved in her own way.

By all means, ask, but leave the other person free.

Those are the four situations in which the Rescue Triangle operates. They form an excellent, practical guide to understand problems about resentment and anger in our lives.

seven

Emotions

The reason we discuss emotions during spirituality conferences is that so often we repress our emotions. As children, when we fall and begin to cry, especially if we are little boys, we are told, "Don't be a sissy; boys don't cry." Sometimes if we are taken to a doctor's office and the big needle is plunged into us, we are told, "This won't hurt!" But the needle does hurt!

What happens is this. Because the child really wants the love of the adult, the child "stuffs" or suppresses what he or she really feels rather than lose that love. Do you wonder why, in later life, a spouse may say, "Don't you have any sensitivity at all, any feelings?" Of course not. From childhood, they have been repressed!

That's why when you train people to deal with spiritual problems, you want to train them to deal with emotions. In the old days, if a person came with a problem, you would deal with it first by getting the person to make an effort, use willpower. Then you would use exhortation, pull out one of your best tapes or speeches. Next there's the use of ideals; you give examples, like a saint, somebody to imitate. You get the person to develop good habits, maybe make out a schedule, a timetable.

If a person came to you with a problem, said she's lazy, then what you would do is use a kind of principle of opposites. Say, "Okay, become industrious." Next you would say, "Look at people who are industrious in the outside world." But, of course, what's happening is that the person feels guilty. A spiritual director may suggest a list of three or four things that a person can do tomorrow and if she gets them done, then he suggests adding a little more, an exercise to do every day. Or he may give an example, a great saint, and with all of this the person may get results, a changed behavior.

However, the person him- or herself is not changed. If you don't change the emotions, you don't change the person.

Today if a person says, "I'm lazy," the question to ask is "You're lazy? What do you mean? There are many kinds of laziness. Describe your own to me." Suppose the person says, "I don't feel a desire to do anything."

"Well, when does it begin?"

"In bed, before I get up."

"Do you feel depressed about it? Was it always like this?"

"No. Only in the last three years."

Something is happening *here, now:* You're becoming aware, and so is the person.

Your subconscious specializes in finding solutions to your most personal problems. Place your faith in it, and give your conscious mind a rest.

—PAUL WILSON, *THE LITTLE BOOK OF CALM*

A basic truth is that all human beings enjoy activity; all humans are loving; all humans enjoy giving. Something has gone wrong somewhere, and the task is to find out what. "No. This has happened only in the last few years."

It may have been "one year after I was ordained a priest."

"What happened? Did something happen?"

"Well, in my last year of studies, everything went well until I failed my final examination. I was supposed to go to Rome. I felt the professors were unfair."

"Are you sure?"

"Oh, yes. What the hell," he says, because he feels there's no career and nothing worth doing.

Go back and find out what is troubling him. You can see he's still angry. But if he truly comes to grips with all of this, he will change.

Today your car breaks down; you and your companion push it. And push it not only to New York City, but to the Bronx. Many people are pushing themselves through their day and through life. No skills required—just tell people to push. However, you need an expert who will lift the hood, check the carburetor, and pour in the gas. That creates change, and the car moves off on its own.

If two people each feel an emotion, somewhere there's a stimulus, an occasion for emotion. And we assume that the stimulus causes the emotion. Nevertheless, your remark does not make me angry. It is my perception of the stimulus that causes the emotion I feel. So your remark may make me angry, while another person stays real cool. If two people wait in a line, one may get uptight while another, quite accepting, remains fully relaxed. Or two people, who have just been told

The art of being wise is knowing what to overlook.

—WILLIAM JAMES

that they have cancer, can react differently. Their way of viewing the situation affects them, and their emotional response is occasioned, but not controlled, by the news. It's harmful not to allow yourself to experience certain emotions: grief, anger, fear, joy, love. These basic emotions have a massive role in making us truly human. By contrast, all other emotions are self-created. Examples: resentment, guilt, jealousy, self-pity, anger at oneself, discouragement, rejection, depression. All these are created by our own thinking, by bad self-talk. Therefore, all can be corrected by our own thinking, by good self-talk.

Anger

All emotions are healthy but can become toxic. Take anger, for example. Most people consider it a negative emotion, one that should be eliminated. Yet it is a very positive emotion. The healthy side of anger is its energy. When you are angry, it is because you want something but are not getting it. You use that energy to get what you want. If you are working hard at something but your work is not recognized and appreciated, and even worse, someone else gets recognition for what you have done, you get angry. Now you use your energy to rectify the injustice.

Expressing your anger is good. Acting out your anger may not be. You can express your anger by closing your car windows and shouting; by beating a pillow; by speaking to the perpetrator of the injustice; or simply by silence, deciding it's not worth making an issue. All these are healthy expressions.

The communicator is the person who can make himself or herself clear to himself or herself.

—Paul Griffith

To act out, to punch someone in the nose, however, is not a healthy expression of anger. We have been taught control, to not show our anger. Different cultures deal with anger differently. Italians are known to express their anger in healthy ways. So expressing it appropriately is a good thing.

Although you've heard it said "The holy man never gets angry," that's not true. Recall the scenes of Jesus in the temple, for example. Anger is one of those negative emotions that we tend to repress, but if repressed, it stores up trouble. Anger is connected with warmth, enthusiasm, self-confidence, but it is also connected with conflict. You have to be wooden if you do not experience and handle your anger. Anger will alert you to situations that call for conflict. This is excellent, because if you can't experience conflict, you can't experience closeness either.

Regarding anger, you have several options. You can feel it, release it, or express it. But don't repress it, or it will do you much harm. You can even scream if that helps you release it. It's an emotion that gets you out into the environment. Yet you must do something to get it out of your system. Maybe you need to go far away and pound a pillow. Such physical releases are especially called for when a person has repressed his or her anger.

Repressed anger is the commonest problem. People who explode often do so because they were all bottled up.

Although repression is bad, suppression is good, and can be wise. I stay aware of my anger but am managing it. I'll find other outlets later. I stay aware of my anger, but it seems good and wise to suppress it now. When you are aware, you are in control. When you are not aware, the anger is in control.

When you really get in touch with your anger, there is nothing to forgive. Married couples often find their feelings toward each other cooling off because they are not open about their negative feelings: "Why rock the boat?" Because they are not able to report those negative feelings, it all builds up. Notice that reporting anger, saying that a certain behavior of yours makes me angry, tells you where I am. And when you become clear where I am, that eases the situation. Sometimes there is no need to reply.

FEAR

The next emotion is fear, which resembles anger. That is, if you repress it, you harden up and create problems. Carl Rogers, a famous psychologist, was the founder of nondirective counseling. One of his clients, an ex-navy captain, had become a taxi cab driver, and now was suffering a paralyzed left arm. His interview with Rogers was filmed, and the client saw excerpts of it.

Later, during an extraordinary session, the kind in which a person blurts out what he'd never say to himself, the man asked Rogers, "Did I ever tell you about the battle of the Philippines? The might of the Japanese navy was there. The first line of ships moved into action, suicide planes making strikes, ships were burning. Then I got the order: Go into action. I thought I'd be afraid, but I wasn't. Moving into battle, I was very calm."

"You were calm?"

"Yes." It was evident that he was reliving the scene. "I feel a tremor now. That's funny. God, I'm moving my left arm!"

What had happened? The man's fear had been frozen all these years. He had not been in touch with his fear, and that's what caused the paralysis.

In World War I, many English soldiers suffered from what was called hysteria. To avoid being called "sissy," they were determined not to show their fear. In the hospital, they were given a drug that helped them relive the battle and experience all the fear. After that, they would calm down.

By contrast, such hysteria was quite uncommon among the French, who could show their fear openly, provided they didn't run away.

So facing our fears is important. Some are natural, normal fears, but others are created by self-talk. We must grow out of these. The conquest of neurotic fear, therefore, is part of growth. I can be relaxed in my own familiar world. Ah, but the vast world outside! I fear strangers, other religions, the dark, speaking in public, risk taking. I also fear being rejected, asking for what I want, giving offense, expressing my odd opinions. Yet to grow means to live on these frontiers, push down the barriers, strike out.

In his own life, Tony de Mello initially feared many things, including mounting the rostrum in a dark room. But "now I speak easily. I delight in the unfamiliar, the unknown."

Some fears need reconditioning. Some of us still fear the dark, for instance. Look at yourself, how you looked as a kid. Talk to that kid. Expose yourself a little to the dark. See how

There is no answer. There has never been an answer. There never will be an answer. That's the answer.

—GERTRUDE STEIN

beautiful it is, really velvety, restful, quiet, peaceful. Perhaps put your head out the window at night, for starters. Later take a few steps outside. After a few days, don't be surprised if you want to visit the local cemetery!

SHAME

John Bradshaw has written and spoken often about the subject of shame. He claims that shame is one of life's most powerful emotions, because it is at the root of all addictions. And like all emotions—anger, grief, fear, and many more—it can be either healthy or toxic.

Healthy shame, Bradshaw claims, gives us permission to be human. It tells us of our limitations, keeps us in boundaries, lets us know we can make mistakes. It tells us we are not God. Therefore, it is a profound source of spirituality.

Toxic shame, by contrast, is healthy shame transformed into a state of being. It takes over my identity. It tells me my essence is flawed, defective. Healthy shame, in one of Bradshaw's best insights, says, "I made a mistake." Toxic shame says, "I *am* a mistake!"

Because it is so unbearable, shame demands a cover-up. So I create a false self. And once I identify with the false self, I cease to be authentic.

Children need models of healthy shame. They should be able to explore, test, cry without their parents, adults, or other caretakers withdrawing love. In his book *Shame,* which I recommend every parent to read, Bradshaw identifies the sources of shame. When he speaks of one source as the family system,

I regard self-esteem as the single most powerful force in our existence. . . . The way we feel about ourselves affects virtually every aspect of our existence: work, love, sex, interpersonal relationships of every kind.

—Dr. Nathaniel Branden

I recall a psychiatrist who told us years ago in a course on pastoral psychopathology about a woman who thought so little of herself, had such low self-esteem, that she was on the verge of suicide. The psychiatrist had difficulty discovering the cause of her malady, especially since she spoke so highly of her mother, who gave her everything: time, attention, affection. But the more he probed, he discovered that the mother, having divorced her husband, gave all her affection to her child. The child had replaced the husband in fulfilling the mother's need for love and affection. The child, even without knowing it consciously, was experiencing herself as a "thing," like a toy, to be used and manipulated, and not being loved for herself. This happens often when parents cannot communicate or express love as adults; they use children to fulfill their own emotional needs.

One helpful solution Bradshaw offers is this: When you experience shame, externalize it. Get it outside of you. Share it with a significant other who is nonshaming. Once again, that is why confession is so helpful in a religious tradition, especially when the confessor is a good spiritual director, a spiritual therapist, and does not allow the person confessing to experience more shame.

Of course, the most powerful tool to heal shame is learning to love yourself. Love yourself unconditionally. Do what Louise Hay in her *Course in Miracles* books suggests when she talks about "mirror work." Look into a mirror frequently and tell yourself you are good! Give time and attention to yourself without resorting to aggression. When you do make mistakes, reframe them.

The most common deathbed regrets relate to neglected relationships, not unfinished business.

—PAUL WILSON, *THE LITTLE BOOK OF CALM*

Here are some thoughts suggested in an article called "Evil and Guilt" by William Yeomans, S.J., from the July 1975 issue of *The Way*.

If by guilt you mean a knowledge or sense that you have done wrong, that is healthy. An understanding, an appreciation that you have harmed another or yourself by not living up to your own reasonable ideals: This is good. But if you "feel" guilty because you have done wrong, if your whole being is consumed by the emotion, you "feel" miserable, awful, and it persists: *That,* psychologists say, is destructive.

Such guilt feelings form a stranglehold grip on your personal liberty. You can even feel guilty about *not* feeling guilty. The latter has a way of killing the relationship of love.

Where there is no love, there is no trust. Feelings of guilt sow a poisonous seed of doubt that kills love. "God will get even with me somehow!"

If people feel guilty about eating steak because of the hungry in Africa or elsewhere in the world, the odds are that they'll expect the hungry to feel grateful to them. They are merely transferring their guilt to the hungry.

Personal guilt feelings can lead to overindulgence toward those about whom you feel guilty. This leads to many a parent's spoiling a child.

Guilt is essentially a "self-centered" emotion. It doesn't focus on the evil, but on what the evil has done or will do to me. Guilt can bog me down in "present-moment immobiliza-

The twenty-first century will be religious or spiritual or not at all.

—ANDRÉ MALRAUX

tion" until I don't like myself, am angry with myself for what I did. I am not okay. It is as if I'm evil, but I'm *not* evil. We must remind ourselves of that often. I am not evil. A father may say to his son, "Son, you did wrong. You stole. Now return the money. You did wrong *and* I love you." And he may even give him a hug.

If morbid guilt is a toxic response, then if I do something wrong and see it as wrong, what is a healthy response?

Answer: repentance and sorrow. Repentance means accepting ourselves with all our possibilities of good and evil. It means abandonment to the forgiving arms of God, who does not reproach or demand an apology. Guilt leaves us scratching an open wound, refusing to let it heal. Repentance heals and strengthens us, setting us on the road to becoming ourselves.

Capturing the loving acceptance of ourselves, by both God and ourselves, banishes guilt forever. That is why in the Christian tradition, the sacrament of penance is considered such a beautiful gift. It is an opportunity to experience the nonreproachful, unconditional love of God. I wonder how many people experience this when they avail themselves of confession.

In the old days, we said that mild guilt is good, but psychological guilt is bad. Psychological guilt means that I'm feeling bad about something that isn't wrong. For example, I arrive late at my father's deathbed. But nowadays we say *all* guilt is bad.

Sorrow and regret, however, are good because it's useful to acknowledge that what you did was wrong, to feel sorrow because sorrow is a sweet, loving emotion. Sorrow, which St. Ignatius called "consolation," makes you shed tears that move

God said, "Ask something of me and I will give it to you."

"I am a mere youth, not knowing at all how to act. . . . Give your servant, therefore, an understanding heart . . . to distinguish right from wrong."

The Lord was pleased that Solomon had made this request. "Because you have asked for this—not for a long life for yourself, nor for riches nor for the life of your enemies, but for understanding—so that you may know what is right, I do as you requested. I give you a heart so wise and understanding that there has never been anyone like you up to now, and after you will come no one to equal you. In addition, I give you what you have not asked for . . . [riches and glory]."

—1 KINGS 3:4–13

you to the love of God. So when you feel sorrow, it's not a negative emotion.

Remember the Spiritual Exercises of St. Ignatius. Jesus comes to us and says, "I know your defects and mistakes, your failures and sins. *And* I love you." The father who forgave his son for stealing doesn't give the boy a guilt trip, nor is God giving us a guilt trip.

Certainly we condemn the actions, but we don't condemn the person. The alcoholic realizes how much damage he has done to his wife and his family. "I'm sorry, Mary," he says with loving tears. However, if he hates himself for drinking, he'll soon be back on the bottle. Don't let him hate himself. Allow people to hate the action if it's wrong, but convey your own great love and compassion to the person.

Of course, apply all this to yourself too. Physician, heal yourself. How can you, given your station in life, have done these wrong things? What a hypocrite you are. So your nice clean record is smudged. You have an ink stain on your First Communion suit. Perhaps you realize you've been a hypocrite all your life. That realization is worthwhile, because if you're able to accept forgiveness from God in your own life, you'll have the power to forgive others. You'll be walking on air, a marvelous help to other people who come to you. Regret the mistake, the sin, and resolve not to do it again, but give yourself a big hug and get on with living. You'll find yourself treating others with new kindliness and friendliness.

Recall the legend about St. Peter: After he denied Christ he went to see Mary, the mother of Jesus, who was in Jerusalem. He poured out his heart. "When I think of all He did for me, he must be very disappointed in me." Of course,

Mary's answer was "Remember, Peter, what He said to you . . . not seven times, but seventy times seven. You know what your trouble is. You need to forgive yourself. Jesus has forgiven you a long time ago."

Speaking of forgiveness, have you heard the joke about a pastor who was leaving on a trip? "If anyone dies while I'm away," the pastor advised, "you'll have to leave them to the mercy of God."

Guilt is selfish and self-centered. It is pride turned on its head. It is regretting not so much the damage as the fact that you are at fault. An example: Once when a factory burned down, a man got the news: total loss and no insurance. When his son came home and found him crying woefully, the young man said, "But, Dad, don't you remember? We sold it last month." His father brightened up. "Oh, well, that's okay now."

CURING GUILT

How do you cure guilt? It is extremely difficult because it's hard to get rid of self-hatred. Let the cure come through a prayer of praise and thanksgiving. Thank God for the evil you have done, all the lapses in your life. Thank God for all that, just as you thank Him for the crucifixion. Thank Him for all of your past. Regret what you have done, but still thank Him.

The words of Juliana of Norwich apply here: "In all manner of things, all shall be well." If you want to use Scripture, take Romans 9–11, the dialogue between the mystic and the theologian. Additionally, God said to Moses, "I will have mercy on whom I wish." So it does not depend on what man wants or does, but only on God's mercy. For God has made all men prisoners of disobedience that He might show mercy to them all. Understand that and you'll be at peace. Experience it and join the dance.

GRIEF

So often in our lives, we fail to grieve. In my own case, I remember when my brother died. Everyone was praising me because I was handling everything so well. I said the Mass, preached the homily, but two years later, when I was in India, Tony de Mello said to me, "I think I know what some problems you've discussed with me are caused by." And I said, "Oh, what's that?" He said, "I believe you haven't grieved enough about your brother's death." I looked at him and said, "Oh, no, you're wrong. Big mistake." So he dropped the subject. But years later I realized that was exactly it. I had never grieved sufficiently. If you don't grieve for somebody, that grief pops up in various ways in your later life. The exercise involves returning to the time when your brother or mother, the loved person, died. Say only "Good-bye, I have to get on with my life."

It's amazing that we can release the emotions by crying. But do it again and again; keep saying good-bye till you feel relaxed.

Because what's happened is your mother or brother died, but emotionally you stayed there. Although you're not getting your love returned, you're unaware of it. When you have been enabled to grieve, then the release comes swiftly.

What can you say to a close friend who is about to die? There is only one thing you can say to give the deepest comfort. Say that in his death, a part of you dies and goes with him. Wherever he goes, you go also. He will not be alone.

—JIDDU KRISHNAMURTI

Animals, you know, do this naturally. In this sense they're extraordinarily spiritual. They rarely kill their own kind; they're never overweight, except the domesticated ones. The mother hen covers her chicks against the eagle hovering overhead. Yet if you see her four weeks later, she's pushing them away, letting them get on with life.

The divinity in nature manifests God. Nature is shot through with holiness. That's why we call life the Big Bible. Look at the birds, the lilies of the field. See the cat when her kittens are taken from her. She grieves for three days but then moves back into life.

Only the human animal holds on to grief, maybe for twenty years. One meets the widow who says her husband is "still enshrined in my heart." No, ma'am, your loyalty is to life; don't waste your life. The ability to grieve and say goodbye is often precious; otherwise, you're in danger of becoming maudlin.

Consider the example of a man who had tremendous love for, and a fine relationship with, his father. But when the man left to become a priest, his father simply swallowed his grief, eventually becoming an alcoholic and dying. Of course, the son assumed he was the cause of all this. So he came to Tony, who suggested some exercises. "I want you to go back in fantasy and talk to your father." Tony got the man to sit in his father's place and talk back to him. Everyone who listened to this was reduced to tears. Mountain-loads of guilt and grief came out. "You're the one thing I loved in life, and then you broke my heart," said the father. Several years later the man told Tony, "I'll never be grateful enough for that hour." Together they had recognized that although death terminates

"When you wake up in the morning, Pooh,"
said Piglet at last, "what's the first thing you
say to yourself?"

"What's for breakfast?" said Pooh. "What
do you say, Piglet?"

"I say I wonder what's going to happen
exciting today?" said Piglet.

Pooh nodded thoughtfully. "It's the same
thing," he said.

—BENJAMIN HOFF, *THE TAO OF POOH*

a life, it does not terminate a relationship. The man had come close again to the one human being whom he'd found losing so painful. Unconsciously this had affected all other relationships in his life.

Try another exercise. Talk to a tree. Make a friend of it. Talk to God, to loved ones. Saying good-bye in the ways discussed here does not mean you'll no longer remember the relationship, but now it will be with joy, love, and gratitude.

Sadly, many people never reach this stage because there's too much unfinished business in their lives.

Ira Progoff's *Intensive Journal* workshops and book also give excellent exercises. Start with the chapter called "Stepping Stones." Learn to say good-bye to people and things. Life is a constant saying good-bye, which will free you to welcome the new.

Don't clutch your precious memories either. Throw them away also. Suppose you've enjoyed a course or a friendship, but now it's over. Accept this, and you will be full of life. The best is still to come. Learn to grieve, to say good-bye not only to persons but to places, things, occupations, stages of growth, to the past. Why then do you go back, recharge those batteries? Not for nostalgic reasons. If self-talk can create bad emotions, then self-talk can *correct* bad emotions. Self-talk can create great good.

JOY

The next emotion is joy. It's strange but true: Joy is commonly repressed. We fear being too happy. Joy resembles love.

One of the most pleasurable exercises around, uninhibited dancing, distracts even the most committed worrier.

—PAUL WILSON, *THE LITTLE BOOK OF CALM*

We're dying to be loved, but we're afraid to let it in. There's a popular superstition: Laugh today and you'll be sad tomorrow. If I allow myself to be full of joy when my friend comes, I'll be sad when he goes. To hold your joy back is not good. Expose yourself to the flow of life.

The amoeba will open fully when pricked, but when pricked three or four times, it does open, but no longer fully. If we were pricked as kids, we too go through life doubled up. We don't grow. When Christ was crucified, He died spread-eagled, open to the world, vulnerable, exposed, which is beautiful. You may be up today and down tomorrow, but underneath lies a deeper peace.

However, you'd rather be in control, so you insulate yourself, and the insulation hides the sparkle. It is gone. Beware of asceticism, of negative attitudes toward the self. Give your body all it needs for pleasure and delight. Enjoy yourself a little more and also you will have no difficulty with sex. A widely spread culture rejects pleasure. There's a folklore that certain jobs are not to be enjoyed, such as being an army general or a CEO in a corporation. So some people don't want to be seen taking a day off.

When Father Jim Gill, S.J., who is a psychiatrist, humorously mentioned this to Pedro Arrupe, the Jesuit general, on several occasions, he regretted that Pedro did not give an example of himself going to the movies or playing the odd game of golf.

The feeling of power can be wonderful, healthy. To be at the tiller is exhilarating. If you have a charisma for your job, enjoy it. You'll do all the better job. Once there was a meeting of all the religious provincials in Goa, India. The food was

Do whatever is necessary to get as much sleep as you feel you need.

—PAUL WILSON, *THE LITTLE BOOK OF CALM*

bad and the mattresses were hard. A picnic was planned by a lovely beach near a Jesuit house, and chilled beer was provided. One man, however, said to Jim Gill, "Do you think we can afford this day?" The poor man worried that, after the grim session on poverty, they didn't deserve a party. Concerned, Jim said to Tony, "Look at their faces. They're all depressed. They need a good break." They needed it and they got it.

Everyone needs emotional and sensory stimulation. Our senses need it. When deprived or caged, animals become withdrawn or overagitated, restless. People who also lack stimulation can suffer from mild depression that is based in repressed anger. You've not been assertive enough, and sometimes you're not even conscious of it. Strangely enough, not taking anger out on others makes people take it out on themselves.

Thus any spirituality that has taught you to be a mouse has created problems for you—problems that cry out for much spiritual help. What you enjoy through touch, sight, taste, feeling—enjoy them fully. Let yourself go. You'd be amazed at how moderate your body is when given its freedom. *Summerhill* by A. S. Neil should be required reading for those engaged in spiritual formation. It's extraordinary. Neil gave students in his school the fullest freedom, knowing there is no better tonic than freedom. Do whatever you want. The only limitation is, don't interfere with another's freedom. Although Neil endured many inconveniences at Summerhill, he found the experience worthwhile. He said, "I don't know of any world religion that is not life-denying." When he gave the kids freedom, he knew they would test to see whether he

The Chinese word for crisis *means "opportunity riding on a dangerous wind." Change has both elements, danger and opportunity. Which do you focus on?*

meant it. The kids' biggest enemy, of course, was their parents, who wanted them to be doctors or lawyers. He said, "I'd rather have a happy street cleaner than a sad doctor." Notice how wild animals eat only what is good for them. But my mother made me eat what she thought was good for me, because children are supposed to meet the needs of grown-ups. Children should be seen and not heard. No! Give them drums. A very quiet child is a very sick child. The parents don't know it because they're proud of the child's good behavior.

Also look at Carl Rogers's book *Freedom to Learn*.

MAKING FRIENDS WITH YOUR BODY

Be kind, loving, friendly, respectful to your body. Treat it kindly and see the results. I'm not talking about being soft, but being friendly. One needs so little to enjoy life to the fullest. But because you have deadened your faculties of enjoyment, you now need alcohol or drugs to get a good feeling. Start getting out into the open again. Blow the dust off all the CDs and tapes that you have hidden away. Listen to them and enjoy. I have an excellent booklet, "Feeling Bad about Feeling Good," by Tom Clancy, a Jesuit. You'll find it in the *Studies of the Spirituality of Jesuits*.

eight

Change

Tony de Mello often said that spirituality is the most practical thing in the world. Why?

Because it deals with your life, your joy, your peace of mind, your serenity, does it rid you of problems, trials, tribulations, difficulties? No. But it does rid you of the heartache, the suffering, the anxiety that usually accompany these.

When the Buddha was asked, "What is it like to be enlightened?" he replied, "Before enlightenment, I was depressed. After enlightenment, I continue to be depressed!"

But with a difference! I don't identify with my depression.

We have to admit that we are asleep. You think admitting that is easy? If you think that denial is present in drug addiction or alcohol addiction, it is present even more so here. We think it funny when we hear the story of the person saying to a woman pushing a baby carriage, "What a beautiful baby!" And the woman responds, "Yes, but you should see the beautiful photos we have at home!" That's a parable of most people's lives. The real baby, real life, reality is right before our very eyes, yet we are running off to look at the "photos."

Know that what the caterpillar calls the end of the world, the awakened person sees as a butterfly.

When Tony was asked why people responded so well to what he was saying, he replied, "Because people are fed up with God-talk. What they want is an *experience* of God." Most people's lives resemble going into a restaurant but never getting to the meal, spending the whole evening looking fondly at the menu.

Then why do we keep *talking* about God if what we really want is an experience of God?

Because we cannot *not* talk about God. He is so much a part of us. Why does a bird sing? Because it has a song in its heart.

However, if we *do* talk about God, one principle should guide us: "Make Him *at least* as good as the best of us." Oh, what we have done to Him! Take, for example, forgiveness. If someone you love dearly offends you and asks for forgiveness, do you say, "On your knees, beg, do penance, then I'll forgive!"? Remember the story of the great Italian painter whose wife was so upset because he wouldn't confess his sins on his deathbed? He told her, "My dear, I am a professional painter. God is a professional forgiver. If He is as good at his profession as I am at mine, I have nothing to worry about." We become like the God we adore. If we make a monster of Him, then we become monsters also.

A radio is an instrument that traps a non-local field of energy and information and creates a space-time event out of it.

—DEEPAK CHOPRA, M.D., *JOURNEY TO THE BOUNDLESS*

Throughout all our religious upbringing and education we are constantly challenged to become better persons. We are encouraged to eradicate our faults, to improve on our virtues. We are given ideals to achieve, lofty goals to strive for, saints to imitate. The struggle for perfection is proposed in vivid detail; the battle between good and evil is clearly outlined in our lives. Although all spiritual masters agree that becoming a better person is surely a worthwhile goal in life, if not an essential part of living, this approach to life takes surprising and enriching turns for different masters.

Do you wonder why Tony de Mello had such a powerful impact on his listeners? He used a simple yet provocative way to approach these crucial spiritual directives in our lives.

When most people think of change, they consider externals—their behavior, for example. "If I would drink less, exercise more, control my violent temper, arouse myself from my laziness," and so on. As helpful as this is, *true* change is always within. It is a matter of attitude. "An absolutely vital fact: the outer world is nothing more than a reproduction of your inner world." As you keep changing, your world keeps changing.

For example, when your own fears have gone, someone you once considered inexcusably rude, you now may see as lonely or terrified. Imagine this absurd drama: A patient explains his symptoms to a doctor. The doctor prescribes medicine for the patient's neighbor. The patient says, "I feel much better now."

What kind of sufferer feels better if only his spouse, or his boss, changes? "The world is right; therefore I feel good." False. "I feel good; therefore the world is right."

Three stages of a person's development:

I believe in Santa Claus.
I don't believe in Santa Claus.
I am Santa Claus.

Where does all the harm come from? Most people think it originates from outside, whereas the actual source is within. All hurt comes from lack of self-understanding. If you have a negative feeling because the rain is ruining your picnic, what is causing the negative feeling? The rain? If someone breaks a promise to you, what causes the negative feeling? The broken promise? Why would someone else not be upset by these events?

Attend to the reason you feel hurt, not to the things or persons who hurt you. Destroy negative attitudes, not negative conditions. Seek first the kingdom. Change or remove the plank in your own eye; then go after the splinter in another's.

The biggest lock on our psychic prison is wanting *control* over ourselves and the world. The result: We become "driven" rather than "carried." When a person lives under the control of an ego that plans, contrives, desires, yearns, demands, dominates, then the inner flow is interrupted. This can lead to alcoholism, psychosomatic illnesses, sexual frustrations, and fear to give these up, lest the person lose control. What do you end up with? Control that leads to loss of control.

Will we ever stop our efforts to burn fire, wet water, add color to the rose? The tremendous message of mysticism: You need not be hurt by anyone or anything inside or outside you. You become like a magician in the midst of a violent crowd who simply becomes invisible when all the sticks and stones are thrown. You aren't hurt. The runaway car can't hurt you while you fly in an airplane above.

When most of us look at ourselves, we always see room for improvement. The ideal of bettering ourselves is always before us, particularly when we see the long history of trans-

*How did Tony de Mello's death affect my life?
As playwright David Mamet said when asked
how his parents' divorce affected him, "You'll
have to ask me when I get over it."*

formation in life: Mary Magdalene, Augustine of Hippo, Ignatius. So it may come as a surprise when you read in a spiritual book a story like "Don't Change" (see Chapter 4; also de Mello, *Song of the Bird,* p. 67). Yes, you are loved just as you are. And if you love yourself as you are, if you see and understand yourself, change for the better will take place automatically. Change is good, crucial. Confucius once said: "The one who would be constant in happiness must frequently change." The secret is to understand how change takes place. It will happen not by effort, not by striving, but by *seeing.*

Of course, we know that when we say "Don't change," we are really invoking a great principle of spirituality: that all the effort in the world, all the striving, all the huffing and puffing will not bring about true change. Not even great intelligence or floods of information (although this can help). Simply look, observe with no comment, no praise, no blame. Do this, and change takes place automatically, effortlessly. Do not turn away. Develop a taste for observation. This, the spiritual masters say, leads us to "openness to change."

PRINCIPLES OF CHANGE

A desire to change is good, healthy. It is energy. Like all desires, we don't seek to fulfill them as much as to understand them. In one of his books, Deepak Chopra remarks that desires, like seeds, contain within them all the mechanics of their fulfillment. All they need is (1) *attention* and (2) *noninterference.*

And how do we interfere? By effort. For example, by pulling on a young plant to make it grow, you destroy it. We

The older I get, the more I see that life is made up of many steps, and they are very small affairs, not great strides.

—DOROTHY DAY

also interfere by becoming rigidly attached to the outcome of our desires. As Chopra said, "One must become more process-oriented rather than goal-oriented." Understand the desire and it will become a "preference." The difference is, I don't make my happiness depend on it. "Congratulations, your wife just gave birth to a baby boy!" "Okay, that was my second choice!"

DIFFERENCE BETWEEN ACCEPTANCE AND RESIGNATION

Acceptance and resignation are not identical. Balzac once said, "Those who resort to self-resignation are the unfortunate people who consummate their misfortune." Acceptance is quite different. I accept the reality but try to change what can be changed. If the reality can't be changed, then I use the misfortune in order to grow. Remember the Serenity Prayer: "God grant me the serenity to change the things I can, the courage to accept the things I can't, and the wisdom to know the difference."

The resigner shrugs his shoulders and says, "That's the way the ball bounces." This is a form of denial, avoidance. Don't go around it, under it, over it, or avoid it by denial, dulling the pain with alcohol, drugs, or useless activity. What's needed is more like grieving: One must "lean into the pain" while getting on with life.

Combine keen desire with acceptance of reality. Talk to the feelings you dislike in a loving, accepting way, and listen to what each has to say. Discover that while the feeling (anger,

During a discussion between the university professor and a monk, the monk starts pouring tea and keeps pouring it till it spills all over. The professor gets up and shouts. The monk says, "Your mind is like that tea cup. It is already full, so there is no room for wisdom."

—JOAN BORYSENKO, *THE POWER TO HEAL*

depression) can do you harm, it also can do you good. Find out its benign purpose. You can accept your feelings without approving of them or resigning to them. Then you are not angry about your anger, you are not depressed over your depression, you are not frightened because of your fears nor discouraged by your discouragement. You can do the same thing with the body's disabilities, your personal shortcomings, past events in your life, external circumstances, old age, and so on. Speak to them with love, and a transformation will take place, not in the world perhaps, but in *you*.

Violence does not lead to lasting change; only love and understanding can.

nine

On Words and Concepts

Here are the ideas that Tony de Mello considered crucial, gathered into one chapter. As with so many themes he treated, much of what appears here he emphasized throughout his conferences.

We all yearn to see how the spirituality of awareness fits into this or that system. Does it all make sense in one context rather than another? Interesting, but of no great importance. The masters say, "Get started and you will see!" There are no adequate words for things spiritual. Only their opposites can be expressed. The guru cannot give truth. Truth cannot be put into words, into a formula. A formula is not reality. The masters point out errors. Drop the errors, and you will know Truth. The common teaching of Thomas Aquinas (who wrote volumes about God) was "About God we cannot say what He is, only what He is not." There is far too much God-talk anyway.

Tony told a fine story about a parachutist who is taken by the wind and ends up hanging helplessly from a tree. Seeing a lone traveler with a mule passing on the road, he shouts down to him, "Where am I?" The traveler replies, "You are up in a tree." The chutist says, "You must be a priest." The traveler is astonished and says, "As a matter of fact, I am, but how did you know?" The chutist answers, "Because what you say is perfectly true, but completely useless!"

But what about the word of God, the Scriptures, those sacred words? We use the words of Scripture so glibly. Worse: If we take them literally without understanding or absorbing them with a "biblical sense," all hell breaks loose. Can you imagine hearing Shelley's "Ode to a Skylark," but not appreciating the metaphorical sense of "Hail to thee, blithe spirit"? Suppose someone complains that a bird isn't a "spirit." How would you deal with the mentality of such a literalist, someone who lacks the understanding and power of metaphor in poetry?

The Scriptures are a hint, indicators, to help you get from where you are to the experience of God you so long for. We all recall the sad story of Galileo, who was indicted, then had his scientific teachings condemned because they contradicted the Scriptures. Galileo held that the planets revolved around the sun, not the reverse, as was believed in his day. Don't the Scriptures say, "The sun rises and sets," which clearly signifies that the sun moves and the earth remains stationary? During the trial, Galileo is said to have asked one of the cardinals to look through the telescope and see for himself that Galileo's

Laziness is nothing more than the habit of resting before you get tired.

—JULES RENARD

teaching was correct. The cardinal refused on the grounds that "it might cause him to doubt" the Scriptures!

Now we consider the fate of women burned at the stake as witches to be a gross miscarriage of justice, a reprehensible act of intolerant, stupid, outrageously bigoted people. When you examine the trials, you find that the reasoning of the perpetrators of these injustices was based on their misunderstanding of the Holy Scriptures. For example: "The branch of the vine that does not produce good fruit should be cut off and thrown into the fire."

Tony used to say that every Bible should have a skull and crossbones on the cover: "Dangerous, read only with great care!" Another insightful observation: Every other page of the Bible should be blank. The purpose being, of course, to show that what is written on the facing page is the Scripture writer's (evangelist's) experience, which is impossible to express in words. What you see in the Bible's words is merely an attempt to describe what God wants the reader to understand.

To mention Thomas Aquinas again, books have been written about his "great silence." In his later years, he had an experience of God while saying Mass. Afterward, he said of all the volumes he had written about God (and upon which the training of priests relics to this day): "All that I have written is as of straw." This "silence" lasted several years. He simply shut up.

The process resembles talking about a papaya without ever visiting Hawaii or having tasted a papaya. You are asked if it is sweet. "Do you mean, candy sweet, ice cream sweet, sugar sweet?" You may write a doctoral dissertation about its sweetness. Now you taste a papaya. "What a fool I've been!" Thomas Aquinas describes how we know God. He mentions that we know him in His creation, in His actions, throughout

Little of England know, who only England know.

—RUDYARD KIPLING

history. But the highest form of knowing Him is *tamquam ig-notum,* to know that one does not know. Later Aquinas even said to know Him as "unknowable."

We are surrounded by God but don't see Him because we "know" about Him. The final barrier to the vision of God is our God concept. We miss Him because we think we "know." Talk about "faith," about taking risks! Try this one: *"I don't know."*

A vigorous example shows the great Christian apologist, C. S. Lewis. When his wife, the woman he adored with all his heart, died, Lewis said his faith, which had been so strong, crumpled like a stack of cards. "Is God a loving father, or the great vivisector?" Sometimes to awaken us to reality, calamity has to strike. Then we may lose our beliefs and come to faith. Lose your childish beliefs and come to adult faith as C. S. Lewis did. "I never had any doubts before about people sur-viving after death until this happened," he said. He talked about hanging from a rope over a canyon. You believe the rope is certainly strong enough to hold your weight . . . until you're in this predicament. Then your certitude becomes shaky. We know nothing about God. Even our questions are absurd. It is like a blind person asking "How many inches are there in the color yellow?" Or "Is it hard or soft?" In India they say, *"Neti, neti!"* ("not that, not that").

KINDS OF AWARENESS

We have so many questions about "awareness," such as "What would it be like to arrive?" A spiritual master was asked, "Is

If people around you will not hear you, fall down before them and beg their forgiveness, for in truth you are to blame.

—FYODOR DOSTOYEVSKY

there some way to summarize in a sentence your teaching about the path to enlightenment?"

The master replied, "I can do it in one word. Awareness."

"But what does that word mean? Can you elaborate?"

"Yes, awareness means awareness!"

The Japanese have a saying, "When you stop, you will have arrived!" Tony de Mello adds, "It doesn't matter!" referring to all the agony over these concepts.

We have talked about awareness of what goes on *in* you, inside this being we call the "self." But there is also awareness of what goes on *around* you. That's why it matters to talk about words and concepts.

Why, when we look at a tree, don't we really see a tree? (When I walk around the parade grounds of Fordham University where I live, there is one tree that I call "my" tree. I stop and speak to it. If I could put my arms around it, I would hug it. I used to think that all that stuff you hear of talking to plants was silly. Of plants getting better when you talked to them. Now I know there is validity in those stories.) Why is it when you look at a person, you don't really see the person? (Have you ever had the experience of trying to converse with someone you find attractive or interesting, but he or she is looking over your shoulder at someone else?)

The reason is that emotions get in the way. Your conditioning. Your likes and dislikes. Your ideas, your conclusions, your concepts. We don't see the person, we see someone or something we've fixed in our minds, an impression. We hold on to that, keep looking at the person through that prism.

An analogy could be drawn with the way the president of the United States, the Pope, or any person in high position gets feedback information in order to run the country or the Church. On one occasion, when John Fitzgerald Kennedy was president, he was asked how he prepared himself to govern when various issues arose. He replied that he read columnist James Reston in the *New York Times* every morning. Half the country went out to buy the *Times* and read Reston. In other words: "Who has the eye—or ear—of these important people?"

Suppose you want to communicate with a loved one but must do it through a third person. Can you imagine how distorted your message would be by the time it reaches the intended recipient? Every pore of your skin, every cell, every sense contributes to this feedback problem.

THE FILTERING PROCESS

That is why it matters to discover who or what is filtering the information you receive. Is it your conditioning? Your culture? Your language?

Words have great power to stir up emotions so that you see things that are not there and respond accordingly. Consider the soldier who is brought to the border of his home country for a final look before he is executed. His heart glows with warm love, his eyes become teary. Of course, his captors have taken him to another border and told him that this is the border of his country.

As you can imagine, the prime villain in the filtering process is attachment.

Great emergencies and crises show us how much greater our vital resources are than we had supposed.

—William James

Thus words and concepts, which so aid communication and science, are often a barrier to reality. Why?

First of all, concepts are universal. For example, I say, "I saw a leaf." But you have the same word for all leaves on the ground (or in the trees), whether big, small, tender, dry, yellow, green, oak, or elm. You have an idea of what I did *not* see: an animal, a shoe, a person. You never find a universal leaf or a human being exactly like your concept. In saying you saw a person, it is true we are all animals, but you have omitted something essential. Besides being a rational animal, you are a particular, concrete, unique woman. The individual can only be experienced, intuited. It cannot be conceptualized.

If you say, "I know Bill. He's a New Yorker," Bill can justifiably be insulted. He can think, "You don't know me. All you've got is a label." Something precious is lost—the person's concreteness, uniqueness. The concept, the word, is not the thing. If you didn't look at things through concepts, you'd never be bored. When you look at a bird, a robin, the robin keeps changing from moment to moment. Thus the concept is abstract, whereas reality is concrete. A concept can help bring you to reality, but when you get there, you must intuit or experience it directly.

Second, concepts are static, whereas reality is flowing. I have the same name for Niagara Falls whenever I see it, but the falls constantly change. How could you invent names for every movement of a river, like the Inuit, who have numerous words for different kinds of snow? How about a gale? Can you capture it in a box, then behold it? Or the flow of a river in a bucket? Or a frozen wave? (Since a wave is essentially movement, action, if you freeze it, you no longer have a wave.)

The third problem is that concepts fragment reality. Consider trying to translate from one language to another. The word *casa* can be translated by "house," but in its original language it means so much more.

Consider the word "tail." Suppose you never saw an animal. How would you understand "tail"?

We fragment the concept "God" continually. As I said, words only point to, indicate, the reality. Once you get there, concepts are useless. As the Hindu priest said to the philosopher, "The ass you mount and use to get to a house is not the means by which you enter the house." To know reality truly is to know beyond knowing.

To paraphrase the anonymous author of *The Cloud of Unknowing:* Go beyond knowing, beyond concepts, words. Poets, painters, mystics, great philosophers have an intimation of this.

Recall my experience of seeing a tree on the Fordham campus. Until you have had this "experience," you might say, "Well, you know . . . tree!" But now I don't see "tree" or what I am accustomed to seeing. I see the object with the child's freshness of vision. There is no word for it. I see something unique, flowing, whole, not fragmented. I am in wonder.

What did you see? There is no word for it!!

Life does not cease to be funny when people die, no more than it ceases to be serious when people laugh.

—George Bernard Shaw

CONCLUSIONS

1. If you have the senses of a mystic, you may get a clue to what I want to say. Suppose I tell a story, write a poem, or paint a picture. If I cannot express this reality that I experience or intuit with my senses, then when I talk about expressing God, what am I talking about? If I cannot express adequately what is visible to my eyes or senses, then when I penetrate or get beyond words and concepts and *see,* how do I express what cannot be seen by eye or heard by ear? When we fall into thinking the word "God" is the thing, we become idol worshippers, worshipping idols made not of wood but by the mind. Mental idols.

2. If you want to escape the prison of concepts, you must look, observe, watch. Look, observe, watch what? *Everything!* Faces of people, shapes of trees, birds in flight. Watch the grass grow! This little exercise is a *spiritual* exercise!

3. Concepts are precious. They help develop intelligence. By means of concepts we are also able to understand the limitations of concepts. So we are invited to become *like* little children, that is, to fall from the stage of innocence, be thrown from paradise, be redeemed. We need to "put off the old man," the conditioned self, and return to the state of a child, yet without being children. Start by looking at reality in wonder—not the intellectual wonder of the would-be mystics, but the formless wonder of the child. Unfortunately, wonder can die as we develop language. But if we are lucky, we return to wonder again.

A friend is someone who knows the song in your heart, and will sing it back to you when you forget it.

—W. N. CLARKE

Every good thought you think is contributing its share to the ultimate result of your life.

—GRENVILLE KLEISER

Dag Hammarskjöld, the former secretary-general of the United Nations, once said, "God does not die on the day we cease to believe in a personal deity. But we die on the day our lives cease to be illumined by the steady radiance, renewed daily, of a wonder which is beyond all reason."

ten

Final Thoughts on Love

Here are a few more of Tony de Mello's thoughts on love. Love is not a feeling. It is ceasing to see the self as separate. I experience you as part of myself. When I experience and love myself, that is not a feeling either; it is the agape-love, whereby I love you and all beings as myself. I am participating in the Creator's love who makes His sun to shine and His rain to fall on all alike; all participate in this kind of love. It involves compassion, feelings. You've also heard it said that love is a decision, and it's certainly a decision on the day you get married for better, for worse, in sickness or in health, in poverty or in riches.

The Good Samaritan's decision to help the unknown Jew is equally impressive. This love is compatible with likes/dislikes, with quarrels, hatreds, the lot. It is combined with universal benevolence. We have attempted to replace this way of loving with willpower. We love everyone with a kind of "plastic love." But if we find negative feelings creeping in, when we'd wanted to be so kind and loving, an element of scrupulosity can arise. That kind of loving is somehow artificial. There's an image of the Buddha, serene, unperturbed, a quiet smile on his lips. This is taken to be holiness. Try to emulate this, and you'll soon feel that you're right back where you started. In the beginning of the spiritual life, trees are trees and mountains are mountains. As you make progress, trees are no longer trees, mountains are no longer mountains. Your whole world is changing. He who was a friend before is an enemy now, and he who was an enemy before is now a friend. Then the time comes where once again, trees are trees, mountains are mountains, and all reality is welcomed.

The genuine holy man or the spiritual person is so ordinary. "I am your divine ordinariness," said one guru with a happy smile. True holiness, true spirituality, is very hard to detect. Holiness is not something put on, superimposed. Difficult feelings are all there, but the person is incapable of damaging anyone. He still has his fears, his anger, grief, love, joy . . . all these emotions remain. The holy man does not withdraw from the human battlefield. He is totally ordinary yet he is totally different. Love is not something produced. It is something given and accepted, and it does not take away your ordinariness or your humanity.

Usually when one speaks of addiction, one thinks of the drug heroin, alcohol, whatever, as the cause. But it is not the drug that is addictive; it's the personality. A nonaddictive personality can take drugs, get high, yet remain nonaddicted.

If one advances confidently in the direction of his dreams . . . he will meet with a success unexpected in common hours.

—HENRY DAVID THOREAU

Don't be afraid to take a big step if one is indicated. You can't cross a chasm in two small jumps.

—DAVID LLOYD GEORGE

What is it that makes people addictive? Is it a lack of love? Is it the fact that they come from broken homes?

No. Studies were made of the GIs who went to Vietnam. Many took drugs, but more than 95 percent of them kicked the habit when they returned to the States. The single quality that tended to make one addictive or not involved *self-confidence*. Without this, the men were most likely to become addicted. If you have a full life and you find your work great, if you have no need to escape or return to the womb, the chances are you will not become addicted. It's the children who grow up in overprotective families who are the likely subjects of addiction. Kids thrown out on their own, on the seat of their pants, are unlikely to become addicted.

In earlier times, coffee was outlawed in some countries. At the turn of the twentieth century, it was spoken of as drugs are today. It seems that when society accepts a drug, there are fewer addicts.

Research has found that another thing can be substituted for a drug, namely a relationship. I mean the kind of relationship when you cannot live without your beloved. You think of that person all day long. Who was it who said, "All love songs are drug songs"?

Many people do not believe this. They've been brought up to believe that another human person is their life. You and I, we can dance together to the same tune, but if you lean on me, you become a burden. The fact is that when you are in *real love,* you're more alive in every area of your life. Love sweetens life. It's not a substitute, which drug love is.

You also can make a drug out of religion. With this substitute religion, this drug religion, when you use Mary, or Jesus, or

I don't do anything that's bad for me. I don't like to be made nervous or angry. Any time you get upset, it tears down your nervous system.

—MAE WEST

God, the effects will be just as bad because you are withdrawing from life, whereas a relationship should open you up. As a result of meeting you, I get interested in gardening, painting, or theater, for instance. When you claim to be interested only in God, read only the Bible, love most of all to be in chapel, I say to you: Be more interested in architecture, music, the newspapers, your business, work, and friends. You are withdrawing from life, which is very bad propaganda for God and His world.

The truly spiritual person does not have to be a witness to anything. A truly spiritual person is totally unselfconscious. A beautiful story illustrates this. "As I parked by the pond, I saw a lotus in full bloom. I instinctively said to her, 'How lovely you are, my dear, and how lovely must be the God who created you.' And she blushed because she had been quite unaware of her great beauty. And it gave her pleasure that God should be glorified. She was the lovelier for being so unselfconscious of her beauty, and she drew me because she made no attempt to catch my eye. Farther on was another pond where I found another lotus, spreading out her petals toward me and saying quite brazenly, 'Look at my beauty and give glory to my maker.' I walked away in disgust."

By all means, cover up your sins, your nakedness, but let your light shine, if it will, utterly unselfconsciously.

The emperor of China was looking for a prime minister. He heard of a holy hermit living in the mountains and sent ambassadors offering him the post. After many days of travel, they came to the place and inquired for him. "Where is the holy hermit?" They climbed a hill and found the hermit sitting half naked on a rock, fishing. They doubted that this could be the man the emperor sought. They made more in-

Because a thing seems difficult for you, do not think it is impossible for anyone to accomplish. But whatever is possible for another, believe that you, too, are capable of it.

—MARCUS AURELIUS ANTONINUS

Whatever you can do, or dream you can, begin it. Boldness has genius, power, and magic in it.

—JOHANN VON GOETHE

quiries in the village, which proved that he was indeed the man. So they climbed up the riverbank and respectfully called to him. After the hermit descended, he received the rich presents and heard their strange request.

When it finally dawned on him that the emperor wanted him to become prime minister of the kingdom, he roared with laughter. He then said to the puzzled ambassadors, "Do you see that turtle down there, wagging his tail in the muck?"

"Yes, respected sir," they said.

"Now tell me . . . Is it true that each of the emperor's household assembles in the royal chapel to pay homage to a stuffed turtle enshrined above the main altar? A divine turtle, whose shell is encrusted with diamonds and other precious stones?"

"It is indeed true, honored sir," said the ambassadors.

"Now do you think that this little fellow wagging his tail in the muck would change places with the divine turtle?"

"No, revered sir," said the ambassadors.

"Then go tell the emperor neither would I. I would rather be alive in these mountains than dead in his palace. For no one can live in a palace and be alive. The day you mount the pedestal and live in the palace, you are dead. Now, do your own thing and I'll do mine."

Beware the multitudes who seek someone who has arrived. If you try to create this illusion, then you get into the sanctity game. The guru game. You can apply this to Christ. Jesus would not be recognized as a guru. "Yet this man, were He a prophet . . ." as you recall. Once they did want to make Him king, but He wasn't to be led astray. He was more like the turtle, wagging his tail in the muck. The disciples were shocked to find him talking openly to a woman. The Pharisees

A driver is a person who doesn't have time to stop for gas, even when he sees the gauge is almost Empty.

—STEPHEN R. COVEY

A man exhausted from sawing a tree with a blunt saw is asked why he doesn't sharpen the saw. His answer: "I'm so busy sawing that I don't have time."

—STEPHEN R. COVEY, *THE 7 HABITS OF HIGHLY EFFECTIVE PEOPLE*

were shocked at the sinful woman's wiping His feet. Jesus never tried to impress anyone with plastic holiness.

Here is Tony's story about how teachers described priests to children. One nun said, "The priest is a representative of Jesus Christ." Afterward, when everyone went out, a six-year-old asked the sister, "Do priests go to the bathroom?" She loyally responded, "Yes, but not as often as other people."

CONTEMPORARY ATTITUDES

Some contemporary attitudes that Tony liked to foster are:

- Freedom from fear and violence
- Adopting friendly attitudes
- Accepting love by recognizing it
- Being in touch with anger, fear, shame, guilt, grief, love, joy
- Nourishing your senses, opening your eyes, ears, heart
- Questioning why/why not?
- Discovering your own truth
- Taking risks, making mistakes, and so being human, vulnerable

Let there be freedom from violence in spirituality, in your interpretation of the Bible, in your attitudes toward sex. Remember this: Whatever brings love, life, joy, happiness, wonder, mystery into your life is prayer.

Note St. Paul's letter to the Philippians (4:8–9): "In conclusion, my brothers, fill your minds with those things that are good and deserve praise. Things that are true, noble, right, pure, lovely, and honorable. Put into practice what you've learned and received from me, both from my words and my deeds, and God, who gives us peace, will be with you."

And from Eric Berne's *Games People Play:* "Awareness means the capacity to see a coffee pot and hear the birds sing in one's own way and not in the way one was taught." It may be assumed, for good reason, that seeing and hearing are different for infants, compared with adults. That infants are more aesthetic, less intellectual, in the first years of life. A little boy sees and hears birds with delight; then the good father comes along, feeling he should share the experience and help his son develop. He says, "That's a blue jay, and this is a sparrow." The moment the little boy is concerned with which one is a blue jay and which a sparrow, he can no longer see the birds or hear them sing. He has to see and hear them the way his father wants. The father has good reasons on his side, since few people can afford to go through life listening to the birds sing, and the sooner the little boy starts his education, the better. Maybe he will be an ornithologist when he grows up.

A few people, however, can still see and hear in the old way. But most members of the human race have lost the capacity to be painters, poets, or musicians and are not left the option of seeing or hearing directly, even if they can afford to. They must get it secondhand.

The recovery of this ability is called *awareness*. Awareness requires living in the here and now, not in the elsewhere, the past or the future. The decisive question is: Where is the mind when the body is here? Consider this in regard to driving to work in the morning. Here are four possibilities. First, the man whose chief goal is being on time is the farthest out. With his body at the wheel of his car, his mind is at the door of his office. So he is oblivious to his immediate surroundings, except as obstacles. This is the fellow whose chief concern is how it will look to the boss. While he drives he almost completely lacks autonomy, and as a human being he is truly more dead than alive.

The second person, the sulk, is not so much concerned with arriving on time as with collecting excuses for being late. Perhaps badly timed lights, poor driving, or stupidity on the part of others fits well into his scheme. He too is oblivious to his surroundings except as they conform to his game, so that he is only half alive. His body is in the car but his mind is out searching for blemishes and injustices.

Third, less common, is the natural driver, the person to whom driving a car is a congenial science, an art. As he makes his way swiftly, skillfully, through the traffic, he is at one with his vehicle. Very much aware of himself and the machine he controls so well, to that extent he is alive.

The fourth case is the rare person who is aware and will not hurry because he lives in the moment with the environment, which includes sky and trees as well as the feeling of motion. To hurry is to neglect that environment in order to be conscious of something still out of sight down the road or of mere obstacles that are solely of one's own making. This final person is alive because he knows how he feels, where he is, when it is. He knows that after he dies the trees will still be there, but he will not be there to see them again so he wants to see them *now* with as much poignancy as possible.

The 7 habits of highly effective people:

1. Be proactive. Pro = not only taking the initiative, but also taking responsibility (to make things happen).
2. Begin with the end in mind. (In computer language, you are the programmer; you create the program; and you work the program.)
3. Put first things first. (It's the fulfillment, the actualization, of habits #1 and #2.)
4. Think win/win.
5. Seek first to understand, then to be understood (empathic communication).
6. Synergize (the whole is greater than the sum of its parts). The relationship that the parts have to one another is a part in and by itself. It is the most empowering, the most edifying, the most exciting part. Applied to marriage, communication, nature, and to the seven habits themselves, it is most fruitful.
7. Sharpen the saw. Renew the four dimensions of your nature (physical, spiritual, mental, and social/emotional).

—STEPHEN R. COVEY

Conclusion

My intention in writing this book has been to present to the reader as much "pure de Mello" as possible. His influence on so many people, including myself, has been profound; this, more than any other reason, is why I wanted to provide for you, the reader, an experience as enjoyable as you would have had if you attended one of his workshops, conferences, or retreats in person.

I not only had the privilege of arranging his conferences in the United States, but of attending almost all of them. I became so familiar with what he taught and the manner in which he presented himself that there grew up within me a "burning desire" to put these thoughts and experiences down on paper for others to share.

Tony and I have had many conversations together over

the years. Having read his books, which I helped publish, and having listened to his tapes, which I was responsible for producing, I feel that I have been faithful to Tony and to his spirit. This book is understandably peppered here and there with my own experiences and ruminations, but even these have been almost entirely influenced by his teaching.

The subtitle of this book, *The Spiritual Themes of Anthony de Mello, S.J.*, could not be more accurate. I owe so much of my own spiritual growth to him and his teaching. It gives me the greatest pleasure to make available to you what I have learned. If anything, this book is a mere token of my admiration, my respect, my love for a brother Jesuit who was a profoundly gifted man and spiritual teacher.

Blessings on all who read these pages.

Epilogue

On numberless occasions I have been asked to say something about Tony de Mello, his life, his work, his death, my personal relationship with him. In the prologue to his book *Way to Love* I wrote about the essentials of this relationship. Let me briefly summarize the heart of those remarks here.

When I first heard of Tony de Mello, it was from Jesuits who had made his eight-day retreat at our Jesuit Retreat House in Annapolis, Maryland. What impressed me most at that time was the fact that he spoke for six hours each day, making a presentation, answering questions, and conducting spiritual exercises (and never used a note). Anyone who could hold the attention and gain the applause of sixty Jesuits certainly intrigued me. I had to hear him for myself. When I did, for only a weekend, I recall saying to myself, "If he can affect me this way in only three days, what would it be like to study with him in India?"

So off I went to Lonavla, India, a lovely rustic spot high in the mountains between Bombay and Poona. At the end of the course, Tony and I had a conversation from which sprang our working relationship. It was an idyllic time for me. I loved hearing him talk to hundreds of conference participants, arranging schedules for the conferences, negotiating the publication of his books, and arranging his television appearances. But, most of all, simply working with him personally gave me a sense of fulfillment and satisfaction that no other apostolic assignment had provided. But it was all soon to crumble like a house of cards. On the morning of June 2, 1987, I found Tony lying dead in his room at Fordham just as we were about to embark on a series of Spirituality Conferences. A heart attack had felled this physical and spiritual giant of a man at the age of fifty-six.

When I gathered the trustees of the De Mello Spirituality Center, which I had created to handle his work, I suggested we close the book and get on with our lives. The trustees disagreed. They felt that I could continue his work. Although I knew his work intimately, no one, I insisted, could walk in that man's shoes—but if his closest friend and collaborator, Fr. Dick McHugh, S.J., was willing to partner with me in offering the conferences, I would be willing to attempt the project.

So, for twelve years, Dick and I traveled the globe—from New York to Los Angeles to San Francisco to Hawaii, to England and Ireland, to Australia, South America, Argentina, and Venezuela. We presented these conferences and continue to do so. Dick is concentrating more on his specialty, "Neuro-

Linguistic Programming," and offers these workshops in Europe, India, and the United States. I have added two members to the team: Jonathan Galente, who has delighted participants with his exercises integrating the de Mello spiritual themes I present in the conferences; and Joan Budilovsky, who offers her expertise in yoga meditation and massage to make our conferences fully holistic. The results and participant reactions have been enthusiastic.★

The De Mello Spirituality Center (legal title: Center for Spiritual Exchange) has offered other specialized conferences, such as an Interfaith Spirituality Conference in Nassau; conferences on spirituality and business; and, in New York, the application of spiritual principles to medicine, involving eminent doctors such as Dr. Deepak Chopra, Dr. Julian Whitaker, and Dr. John Sarno. So the work goes on.

★Along with the conferences, the Center distributes all of Tony de Mello's books, audiotapes, and videotapes of TV presentations.

Bibliography

Berne, Eric. *Games People Play*. New York: Ballantine, 1996.

Bradshaw, John. *Healing the Shame That Binds You*. Deerfield Beach, FL: Health Communications, Inc., 1988.

————. *Homecoming: Reclaiming and Changing Your Inner Child*. New York: Bantam, 1992.

Chopra, Deepak. *The Seven Spiritual Laws of Success*. San Rafael, CA: Amber-Allen Pub., 1995.

————. *The Seven Spiritual Laws*. New York: Crown, 1999.

de Mello, Anthony. *Awakening: Conversations with the Master*. Chicago: Loyola Press, 1998.

————. *The Heart of the Enlightened*. New York: Doubleday, 1989.

————. *More One Minute Nonsense*. Chicago: Loyola Press, 1993.

————. *One Minute Nonsense*. Chicago: Loyola Press, 1993.

————. *One Minute Wisdom*. New York: Doubleday, 1988.

————. *Praying Body and Soul: Spiritual Living in a Secular World*. New York: Crossroad, 1997.

————. *Sadhana: A Way to God, Christian Exercises in Eastern Form*. New York: Doubleday Image, 1984.

————. *Song of the Bird*. New York: Doubleday, 1982.

————. *Taking Flight: A Book of Story Meditations*. New York: Doubleday, 1990.

————. *Way to Love: The Last Meditations of Anthony de Mello*. New York: Doubleday, 1995.

————. *Wellsprings: A Book of Spiritual Exercises*. New York: Doubleday Image, 1986.

Hanh, Thich Nhat. *Teachings on Love*. Berkeley, CA: Parallax Press, 1997.

Lamb, Albert, ed. *Summerhill School: A New View of Childhood*. New York: St. Martin's Press, 1993. (Originally published as A. S. Neill, *Summerhill: A Radical Approach to Child Rearing*. New York: Hart Company, 1960.)

Progoff, Ira. *At a Journal Workshop: Writing to Access the Power of the Unconscious and Evoke Creative Ability*. New York: Dialogue House Library, 1975; reprinted Tarcher Putnam, 1992.

Robbins, Anthony. *Secret to Wealth and Happiness*. New York: Simon & Schuster, 1999.

————. *Unlimited Power*. New York: Simon & Schuster, 1997.

Stroud, J. Francis, S.J., ed. *Awareness, A De Mello Spirituality Conference in His Own Words*. New York: Doubleday Image, 1992.

Wilson, Theodore A. *D-Day, 1944*. Lawrence, KS: University of Kansas Press, 1994.

About the de Mello
Spirituality Center

The Center for Spiritual Exchange, the legal title for the de Mello Spirituality Center, is a not-for-profit organization incorporated in the State of New York to carry on a variety of programs in the spirit of Father Anthony de Mello. This involves the study and discussion of the intellectual, psychological, and cultural foundations of value systems, drawing on insights of contemporary psychology, anthropology, sociology, and the arts. It involves also the presentation of these findings through face-to-face seminars, conferences, and classes and through all communication media, especially film, radio, recordings, and television.

For information on future conferences and to order books, audiotapes, and videotapes, write or phone:

Father J. Francis Stroud, S.J.
de Mello Spirituality Center
Fordham University
Faber Hall
Bronx, NY 10458–5198
Tel. (718) 817–4508
Fax: (718) 817–4518
E-mail: jstroud@cyburban.com
Web page: www.demello.org

J. FRANCIS STROUD, S.J., is the executive director of the de Mello Spirituality Center at Fordham University, which produces books, videocassettes, and audiotapes on the teaching of Anthony de Mello.